"Brother Lawrence can teach us much if we have a hunger for a deeper spiritual life. Steve Case helps us to learn what this saint of bygone days can offer us. I found this little book inspiring, challenging, and incredibly thought-provoking."
—TONY CAMPOLO, Ph.D., professor emeritus, Eastern University, St. Davids, Pennsylvania

"The highly accessible images, metaphors, and insights of Steve Case bring the words of Brother Lawrence to twenty-first-century life! If you've ever doubted that it's possible, outside of a monastery, to remain fixated on God every moment of every day, this book will transform that skepticism into shattering conviction. *God Is Here* is, quite simply, brilliantly illuminating."
—Karla Yaconelli, owner/CEO, Youth Specialties

"Many of us devote only a minimal amount of our day to spiritual contemplation. For Brother Lawrence, however, God's presence pervaded every moment of the day. Steve Case, through his immersion into the story of this great saint's life, reminds us that the presence of the Divine surrounds us continually, and he teaches us how to tap into that presence. *God Is Here* is the book to read for those who want to move more deeply into the spiritual life."
—MARY BLYE HOWE, author, *A Baptist Among the Jews* (Jossey-Bass) and *Sitting with Sufis* (Paraclete Press)

"As long as I've known him, Steve Case has demonstrated an uncommon ability to communicate vivid imagery, rich spiritual insight, and gut-level emotion through the written word. And that's exactly what you get with *God Is Here*. Case's insightful commentary on Brother Lawrence's timeless spiritual wisdom is at-once humorous, engaging, disarming, and deep—a breath of much-needed fresh air."
—DAVE URBANSKI, senior developmental editor, Youth Specialties; author, *The Man Comes Around: The Spiritual Journey of Johnny Cash* (Relevant Books)

"I stumbled on *The Practice of the Presence of God* a few years ago and was immediately captivated by the simplicity and depth of Brother Lawrence's teachings. I have gone back to the book many times since. I'm glad that someone like Steve Case has picked it up and dusted it off for the next generation, taking Brother Lawrence's words and using them as a jumping-off place to discuss connecting with God. Like Brother Lawrence, Case has aimed for simplicity and depth. I think he hit his mark. This is a great book for young Christians and for those who have been away from the faith for a while and feel a drawing to come back home."
—ERIC HURTGEN, God section editor, RELEVANTmagazine.com

God Is Here

God Is Here
Connecting with Him in Everyday Life

Steve Case

[RELEVANTBOOKS]

Published by Relevant Books
A division of Relevant Media Group, Inc.

www.relevantbooks.com
www.relevantmediagroup.com

Design by Relevant Solutions
Cover design by Greg Leppart
Interior design by Jeremy Kennedy

Relevant Books is a registered trademark of Relevant Media Group, Inc., and
is registered in the U.S. Patent and Trademark Office.

Library of Congress Control Number: 2005902185
International Standard Book Number: 0-9763642-4-7

For information or bulk orders:
RELEVANT MEDIA GROUP, INC.
100 SOUTH LAKE DESTINY DR. STE. 200
ORLANDO, FL 32810
407-660-1411

05 06 07 08 9 8 7 6 5 4 3 2 1

Printed in the United States of America

For Aprille and Eric.

This book is dedicated with love to my two children:

Aprille, who has a passion and a thirst for knowledge that is unrivaled. She has a better sense of the big picture than I have ever seen in any sixteen-year-old EVER. Since she was old enough to walk, she has known exactly when I needed a hug.

Eric, who is unquestioningly the bravest person I know. He has the ability to look incredible adversity right in the eye and tell it a joke. Since he was old enough to talk, he has known exactly when I needed to laugh.

They are both the reason I do what I do and the inspiration.

Love,
Dad

Contents

Acknowledgments

Special thanks to:

Beth Slevcove, who said, "Have you ever read Brother Lawrence?"; *www.carmelite.com* for additional information; Cara, Jeff, Cameron, and the rest of the Relevant staff, who believed in this project, and especially to Tia, who slogged through pages of muck to help put this book into a coherent thought; Becky, for understanding and patience beyond understanding.

Preface

The Vision of Brother Lawrence

Nicholas Herman trudged through snow up to his knees. There was a cold wind that seemed to blow through his coat and tunic and seep into his skin. He was cold. His feet were freezing. Nicholas was never a graceful man to begin with, but walking in deep snow made his awkwardness all the more annoying.

Falling again, he raised himself up and adjusted the scarf around his neck. Barely eighteen, he trudged from the church where he had been visiting with Father Lawrence. The old priest had looked well. Father Lawrence had been Nicholas' only teacher. Nicholas had never been to school. All his education had come from his parents or from the good father. The young man had not cared for his lessons as a boy, but he loved and respected the old priest and had visited him when he was home. Nicholas would be going off to war soon, and he didn't know if he would ever have a chance to see his friend again.

Standing still for a moment, Nicholas breathed heavily, slowing himself; the journey through this sort of cold was never one of speed but of slow, constant progress. He stared ahead of him at a tree, stripped bare of its leaves by autumn and now hanging with icicles on its branches. He became suddenly aware of the silence around him. There was no noise in the air. The town seemed quiet. Singing from the nearby children's school ceased. Even the wind had stopped blowing, leaving Nicholas with a profound sense of silence.

Nicholas looked around and then once again at the tree. In his mind he saw the most incredible vision. Icicles began to drip, melt, and fall away from the branches. The bark of the tree, black and old, began to grow and turn a healthy brown. The ends of the branches began to move, though there was no wind, and the tiniest of leaves sprouted and grew, and in a matter of seconds every twig of every branch sported a new green leaf. Each new bud, each new sprig of green made an audible pop as if it had been held under and then was suddenly released. The leaves turned from green to yellow to orange until the tree looked as though it were on fire. Buds nearly burst out of the branches and, like the leaves, grew quickly until they became apples. Each one was full, ripe, and red. The eighteen-year-old fell to his knees in awe. Was this happening? Really happening? Was it in his mind? Was it a vision from God? The tree that only moments ago was bare and withered now stood in full autumn. The sun was behind a winter cloud, yet the tree grew still warmer and brighter. Nicholas felt this warmth and then realized it was not coming from the sunless sky. The warmth was from within him. He parted his scarf and opened the top button of his coat, allowing the warmth to soothe him. The warmth in his chest spread through his body and became a kind of joy. He laughed out loud, knowing full well that if anyone saw him opening his coat and laughing at a broken winter's tree, they would think him insane, yet he didn't care.

The apples now grew fuller and larger and began to drop off the branches and disappear into the snow beneath. The leaves grew brown and fell and were blown away by wind that only the tree seemed to feel. The branches, now bare, again turned black, and the light that had illuminated the tree faded, leaving the young man still standing in the snow with his coat undone. Nicholas was still too amazed by the sight to be saddened by its ending. He looked again at the bare tree in front of him and then realized the warmth that had overtaken him in the vision had not faded with the leaves on the tree. His heart and body were warmed, though his skin now began to chill. As he pulled the coat over his chest, he felt joy surge through his body. He laughed out loud again. He knew that God had shown him something. He knew that this was a vision. He knew that like the tree that had just passed through all of the seasons in a matter of moments, he too was going to change. He was filled with the hope that God had smiled on him and had told him something ... shown him something.

How to know good from bad?

Nicholas stood and began to walk toward his parents' house again, still laughing to himself, still feeling the warmth of the presence of God within him. He did not know yet what this vision meant, but he knew one thing. He didn't want this feeling to end. He dedicated himself then and there to walk in the presence of God for the rest of his days.

Author's Note:
Certain parts of the biography have been "dramatized" based on the available facts. There is no place in the Bible that says the Pharaoh's palace smelled like dead rotting frogs, but since the Bible says it recently rained frogs before Moses' visit, the smell is something we can assume and can be added when we tell the story of Moses. The "dramatized" portions of this book work that way.

Introduction

A Note from the Author

As I began the process of writing this book, I discovered that most people react to the name Brother Lawrence in one of two ways. They either say, "Who?" Or they say, "Ohhhhh, yeah. I love Brother Lawrence." There has been no middle-of-the-road reaction. People either love his work, or they have never heard of him.

I wanted to write a book that would appeal to both crowds. If you have never heard of Brother Lawrence, undoubtedly you have turned to this introduction for the gist of what this book is about. Perhaps something about the cover or the title intrigued you, or maybe you are standing in a bookstore wondering about your faith and are looking for something spiritual that doesn't club you over the head with the Scriptures.

You turned to this page to read just a little. (You can skip to chapter 2 if you want. It will give you a better idea of what's in store for you.) If you are already a fan, you've probably started here because you bought the book as soon as you saw the words "Brother Lawrence" on the cover. There are not many books out there about Brother Lawrence and his work; hopefully you will enjoy this one.

I came to know the work of Brother Lawrence through a small slip of paper. I found it in my L.L.Bean carry-all bag. It said "Brother Lawrence. Monk. Kitchen. Check it out." It was my own handwriting. I'm used to this. I talk to a lot of people at conferences and seminars, and frequently people recommend books to me. I jot down the title and slip it into my wallet or drop it in my bag and then find it months later. This recommendation came from a woman named Beth at a youth ministers' convention. I have little memory of the conversation, but I do remember her talking about Brother Lawrence and writing myself the note, but what "kitchen" and "monk" had to do with it, I had no idea.

I went to Amazon.com and found the shipping cost to be more than the actual book, so I bought it. I put it on my bookshelf, vowing to get to it after I finished the many books I was already reading. Months later I was carrying a cup of coffee around and looking for something to read on my back porch. (I have found that my back porch has a sort of "seal" around it where I cannot hear my computer calling me to work, the kitchen calling me to load the dishwasher, or my dryer calling me to fold the towels. I like my back porch.) Coffee in hand and feet on the chair across from me, I started to read. I finished the book that same day. That coffee on that back porch was part of the chain of events that eventually led to the book you are holding in your hands now. (I hope that you have a cup of coffee and are sitting in a quiet place that you enjoy as well.)

I became one of the many thousands of people who read the words of a humble monk, written in the seventeenth century, and was forever changed.

I picture Brother Lawrence as a surfer. There is absolutely no evidence out there to suggest that Brother Lawrence ever surfed, yet that is how I picture him. More accurately, I picture him walking along the beach with a surfboard or perhaps leaning against it while sleeping and letting the wind come in off the water and blow his hair. I picture him talking to surfers and shell-collecting tourists and old guys with metal detectors, all who stop and have a brief conversation with a man who seems wholly content in his own skin.

Brother Lawrence was a man of peace. Perhaps a man of "peacefulness" is a better way to describe him. Those who wrote about him said he was a man of good humor and kindness; he always seemed at peace with himself.

Most of the world only knows Brother Lawrence through a small book called *The Practice of the Presence of God*. While Brother Lawrence never sat down to write a book, friends and colleagues compiled a collection of his writings, letters, and notes from personal conversations into a collection and published it. It is not much writing, but this small bit of wisdom has been translated into many languages and has touched the lives of millions.

We are lucky we have this much. Brother Lawrence was said to have disliked trying to write about his experiences in being in communion with God. Often he would write things down and then, when reading it back, would decide that it was not even close to describing the joy and peace he felt. He often destroyed his own writings and vowed not to attempt again.

However, Brother Lawrence chose to keep writing, and the result was a simple and beautiful explanation of how to continually walk with God. He desired no material blessings and found peace and tranquility in whatever he did because he was connected to God in all things and at all times.

There are two more reasons I like Brother Lawrence. One, he was a cook, although working in the kitchen was painful to him. He often returned to help in the kitchen even when he was assigned to other duties in his later years. In fact, he often said that he saw little difference between the time the monastery set aside for prayer and the time he spent in his kitchen. I like to cook. I like Thanksgiving dinner. Every burner has a pot, the microwave is humming, and the oven has three or four items crammed in. Things are boiling, baking, and browning, and it's all timed to be done right when the timer on the stove goes off. That's a beautiful thing for me. (Cleaning up is another matter entirely. Brother Lawrence spoke of that too, but we'll get to that later.)

History also tells us that Brother Lawrence was a footman and, for a brief time, a soldier, but also that he was, in his own words, "a great awkward fellow who broke everything." Being a great awkward fellow myself, I tend to feel a certain kinship with other great awkward fellows.

It was this kind-hearted man whom I met in the pages of his writings. In the midst of the clatter and chaos of my life, I met this "great awkward fellow" who taught me about not about "finding" God but about "acknowledging" that God was already present. That God was already closer than my skin and that I just had to "connect" to it.

This book can change you. It will not make you a person like Brother Lawrence. I've read Brother Lawrence's book many times and cannot seem to come close to that sense of inner peace and contentment with the world around me that he felt. But I have been changed by him. I have found a way to let the world and the little things bother me less.

In addition, Brother Lawrence wrote quite a bit about getting rid of worldly things, and I'm not quite willing to let go of Krispy Kremes, Ben & Jerry's, my email, my Converse All Stars, and my ... well, you get the idea. If there is a sense of peace out there that comes from God and is present all the time, then I have tapped into it. Perhaps I am on the outer edge. Maybe this book will bring you a little closer. Maybe it can hold the door for you, and you can keep going from here.

01

A Biography of Brother Lawrence

The fifty-four-year-old monk was most surprised by the cold. Rarely was he out of his kitchen at this time of morning. He smelled the smoke from the fires, and if he listened hard, he could hear the chanted prayers of his fellow brothers. He had been excused from both the kitchen and the prayers this morning. He did not miss the noise and heat of the kitchen, but he missed the sense of safety that goes along with routine. He sang along with the chants as best he could and prayed silently. Beyond the village he could see the sky begin the slow process of changing color as the sun came up.

He stopped a moment, feeling an almost childlike anticipation for what he was about to do. There were times as a child when his father had told of long journeys they were going to take, and he had scarcely slept the night before. Last night he lay awake long into the darkness thinking of this journey and what he might see, praying that God would watch over him.

*Upon feeling this childlike giddiness, he laughed out loud.
The sound of his own laughter made him feel even less like
an old monk and more like a child, and he laughed harder
still. The thought that one of his fellow brothers might come
out and see him laughing all by himself tickled him further
still. The only eyes that saw him belonged to the horse that
turned and simply looked at him. Brother Lawrence patted
the animal's neck and continued to sing in a loud voice
even though the prayers from the sanctuary had ceased.
In the dim light of the morning, he could see not just the
hot breath of the horse but the steam that rose from the
animal's body. The monk thanked God for His creation and
that he would not have to walk the five hundred miles to
Auvergne.*

*He hitched the horse up to the wagon and laid the reins
across the seat. It would take him awhile to climb on
board. He never asked for assistance though others
had offered. His leg pained him greatly, especially on
cold mornings. It often felt like dead weight that he was
dragging around until he turned too quickly, stepped too
far to the side. Then the pain was intense, but he did not
complain. He imagined the bullet was still somewhere in
his thigh, and he thanked his Creator that it had not taken
his entire leg or his life.*

*The boatmen who brought the wine in barrels marveled at
the monk's upperbody strength. Brother Lawrence was a
large man, his frame made bigger by the robe. Were it not
for his leg, he probably could have loaded the wine onto
the wagon himself. Instead he had to assist the boatmen as
best he could before traveling back.*

The journey would take three weeks and would mark his first trip out of the monastery in almost a quarter of a century. Grasping the side of the seat board on the wagon and carefully placing his good leg on the step, he hoisted himself up into the seat in one motion. He winced at the pain that shot through his leg. Getting himself seated, he physically pulled his other leg into the wagon with his hands. He put it in place next to the other one and bent it. He waited for the pain to subside. When it did somewhat, he picked up the reins. He turned back to look at the monastery and said a prayer asking God's blessing on his fellow brothers and on the journey that lay ahead of him. With a flick of the reins and a quiet command, the horse began to move, pulling the empty wagon behind.

Brother Lawrence was born with the name Nicholas Herman in 1611. (There is some discussion as to the actual date, but most scholars believe it was close to this year.)

He was born in Hérménil near Luneville in Lorraine, France. Very little biographical information is known about his childhood. His parents saw to his education with the help of a parish priest and probably covered the elementary levels. Nothing is known of his secondary education or his job. He does write about a profound spiritual experience he had in his eighteenth year, which changed the course of his life, though he did not take his vows as a monk until more than a decade later.

He became a soldier during the Thirty Years War, a highly vicious time in history. Though Nicholas never wrote about or described that time of his life, reports of lootings and atrocities have been documented. Brother Lawrence later referred to "the disorders of his youth," the "sins of his past life," and his determination to "rectify past conduct."

During his time in the service, he was captured by German soldiers and accused of being a spy. He was held captive and told that he was going to be put to death. The young man talked his way into a release. Think about that last sentence. Soldiers have captured what they believe is a spy for the other side, and he simply talks his way out of the charges. It is hard to imagine what that conversation must have been like. The German soldiers must have seen something inside him that compelled them to let him go. Perhaps it was that inner light that Brother Lawrence said remained with him and inside him until his death. Who knows? They released him, and he rejoined his troops.

During the battle of Rambervillers in 1635, Nicholas was wounded in the leg and had to return to his parents' home. It was a wound that would cause him great pain and plague him for the rest of his life.

After leaving the service, Nicholas attempted to lose himself in the wilderness and became a hermit. That didn't last long. He became the personal valet to the treasurer of the king of France. In his own writings Nicholas referred to himself as being "clumsy" with a tendency to "break everything." His employment did not last.

In 1640 Nicholas joined the Order of Discalced Carmelites on the Rue Vaugirard in Paris. In August of that year he received the brown robes of the Carmelite and took the name Lawrence (perhaps recognizing the priest who had taught him when he was younger). He completed the name with "of the Resurrection."

Brother Lawrence of the Resurrection went into what he called a "dark time." He believed that, when he became a monk, God would heal him of his clumsiness and of the pain in his leg. When this did not happen, Brother Lawrence believed he was lost, that he would be damned forever as a result of his past life, that he would be "skinned alive" for his sins. Believing that he was not good enough, not devoted enough, not pure enough, Brother Lawrence sank into a depression that would last a decade. He dwelt only on his past, thinking that "all creatures, reason, and God Himself were against me."

Brother Lawrence wrote:

> When I thought of nothing but to end my days in these troubles, I found myself changed all at once; and my soul, which till that time was in trouble, felt a profound inward peace.
>
> As for what passes in me at present, I cannot

express it. I have no pain or difficulty about my state, because I have no will but that of God, which I endeavor to accomplish in all things, and to which I am so resigned that I would not take up a straw from the ground against His order, or from any other motive than purely that of love to Him.

He was assigned the job of cook, where he worked for the next fifteen years, until he could no longer stand for long periods and was assigned a job where he could sit and became a sandal maker. By this time his order had grown to more than one hundred Carmelites and a larger number of young men in training.

He was also given the job of purchasing wine even though he often said he had no head for business. He made two trips out of the monastery to buy the wine. The first, a five hundred-mile journey to Auvergne. And a second to Bourgogen, which had to be done by river. So handicapped was he by this time that the only way he could move about the boat was by rolling over the barrels.

It was the rule of the Carmelites that there was to be a distinction between work time and prayer time.

"Each one of you is to stay in his own cell or nearby, pondering the Lord's law day and night and keeping watch at his prayers unless attending to some other duty."
—The Rule of Saint Albert, Chapter 8

Brother Lawrence found a way to make his prayer and his work become one and the same.

He sat on the bench that a fellow monk had built for him. It was wider on the side of his aching leg, so that when he sat, his thigh had more support under it, easing the pain somewhat. The bench had no back, but this position allowed Brother Lawrence to work on the sandals in front of him. His eyesight was beginning to fail, and he often moved the bench closer to the window in the daytime. In the early hours after the morning prayer, he would often look up from his work to see the city come alive.

Sometimes the children would wave, and he would wave back. During the years after his last purchasing trip, Brother Lawrence became known as a man of great peace and of great wisdom. He found that he had company in his sandal shop nearly as much as he was alone, though he personally never considered himself to be alone and would often talk to God for hours as he repaired the sandals of his fellow monks.

"Brother?" a voice said.

Brother Lawrence looked up. "Jean Jacques," he said, smiling to see his friend and frequent visitor. "It is good to see you."

"I was delivering the bread," the young man said. He was wearing an apron that looked as though, from the copious amounts of flour, that Jean Jacques had been baking bread all night.

"How is the baby?" Brother Lawrence asked.

"She cries a lot," the young father replied. "So much that I cannot sleep, and I go down to the shop and have much of the baking done before the sun comes up."

"Her cough?"

"Gone," said the baker. "I have been praying all the time, so has my wife, and the baby is breathing much easier."

Brother Lawrence smiled. "May God grant you some sleep before too many days pass."

The baker crossed himself and bowed in gratitude. "May God grant me sleep now because I do not think I will be sleeping if she grows to be as beautiful as her mother."

Brother Lawrence laughed one of his loud, contagious laughs, and his whole body shook. The pain shot through his leg and into his back, but he continued to laugh.

The young baker bowed again, placed his hat on his head, and went out the door. Brother Lawrence watched him from the window and chuckled at how the wind seemed to create a cloud of flour in the father's wake.

Brother Lawrence returned to his work. Brother Philippe was on his third pair of sandals in a year. He had massive feet, and his arches caused the sandals to wear unevenly; consequently, he found himself falling down a lot when he stood up from kneeling.

He chuckled at the thought of Brother Philippe, who, when he lost his balance, waved his arms in the air frantically.

Brother Lawrence was expecting his regular visit from Monsieur Beaufort, the grand vicar to Monsieur de Chalons (formerly the Cardinal de Noailles). Monsieur Beaufort always brought sheaths of paper and ink pens and kept notes of their conversations as if he were going to be tested on them later.

Rich and poor, old and young, educated and simple—all found that a conversation with Brother Lawrence was most rewarding. Even a bishop of France would occasionally come to visit with the humble sandal maker. For more than fifty years Brother Lawrence prayed and conversed and shared his ideas on the practice of the presence of God.

He was frequently sick during the last years of his life, but he was never unhappy, never complaining. His only complaint was to his doctor, to whom he said, "Doctor, your remedies have worked too well for me. You have delayed my happiness."

In a letter written just a few days before he died, Brother Lawrence said,

> *Let us begin to be devoted to Him in good earnest. Let us cast everything besides out of our hearts. He would possess them alone.*

Beg this favor of Him. If we do what we can on our parts, we shall soon see that change wrought in us which we aspire after. I cannot thank Him sufficiently for the relaxation He has vouchsafed you. I hope from His mercy the favor to see Him with a few days. Let us pray for one another.

Brother Lawrence died on February 12, 1691.

But his work and words have never died.

02

God of Pots and Pans

This ain't no prayer of Jabez:

Lord of all pots and pans and things ...
Make me a saint by getting meals
And washing up the plates!

The words of a seventeenth-century Carmelite monk, who prayed, drank wine, made sandals, and worked in the kitchen.

We went a little Jabez crazy a few years back, didn't we? An obscure little prayer from the book of 1 Chronicles was repackaged, and suddenly the world was praying for an increase in territory and for even more blessings from God.

Jabez asked for blessings upon himself.

Oh, God, bless me indeed and expand my territory.

The Bible tells us that God answered Jabez's prayer. It's possible that God blessed Jabez for having had to grow up with a name that means "son of pain." Your mother may hold labor over your head, but at least she didn't name you "hard labor." Jabez grew in reputation. He was a good man. He asked, and God gave him what he wanted.

Brother Lawrence asked only to feel God's continued presence. He did not ask for God to show Himself. He already believed God existed. He did not say, "God, let me find you." Or "God, come to me." He believed that God was already there. He only asked that God stick around, to feel that presence.

The value of his teachings lies in his modesty and his simplicity. Brother Lawrence had no desire for fame, fortune, or even recognition. He preferred to live quietly and believed that he had found the way to be "in the presence" all the time. With this, he felt he needed nothing else.

"The time of business," he wrote, "does not with me differ from the time of prayer, and in the noise and clatter of my kitchen, while several persons are at the same time calling for different things, I possess God in as great tranquillity as if I were upon my knees."

Most of us would be happy to feel that connection when we prayed, let alone to feel that pure joy every moment of every day.

The one prayer that he is known for may sound like something you'd read on a potholder found at a Christian bookstore, but it is, in essence, what Brother Lawrence was all about.

These three lines sum up a life and way of life and capture the essence of a man's faith. Most of us could not sum up our life mottos in less than a page.

Lord of all pots and pans and things ...

Pots and pans?

This is the Father of all creation we're talking about. To think of Him as the God of pots and pans is like looking at the ceiling of the Sistine Chapel and talking about the paintbrushes. Yet this is the essence of the lessons of Brother Lawrence. This is the essence of practicing the presence of God.

We tend to believe we must seek God on the grand scale. We have to see the hurricane. We have to be there in the Sistine Chapel. We have to stand as one of thousands at the Christ-A-Palooza Music Festival in order to feel that presence.

Brother Lawrence disagreed. He said that God is in the pots and pans and things ... that the time of prayer is no different than the time of action. Everyday actions are prayer.

I have a tendency to let the dishes go. I tell my wife

that it's because I worked in the cafeteria dish room when I was in college, so one meal's dishes just is not enough of a challenge for me.

There is no difference between scrubbing dried Fruity Pebbles off a bowl and singing an aria by Bach.

We hold those people who can lift the rafters in high regard. We look forward to the Sundays when we hear them sing. We count on those moments to make ourselves feel closer to God. The King's Singers, the Bach chorales, Saint Paul's Men and Boys' Choir ... wonderful, glorious church music that lifts the soul and sends it soaring with the voice.

Brother Lawrence said that we should be able to connect with God just as well as if we were cleaning the sanctuary instead of sitting in it listening to the music.

It involves setting your mind and heart on the right connection. This sounds difficult, but we do it all the time. There are movies we go see simply because we want to escape for two hours. We want the popcorn and the watered-down Cherry Coke, and we sit at the back so that the audience's reaction is part of the experience. Or we can go see a film that "everyone is talking about." It has "great social relevance." We do not have the same mindset for those films. We do not buy popcorn to see *Schindler's List* or Mel Gibson's *The Passion of the Christ*.

We change the setting on that dial in our minds. You do it all the time, without thinking about it. You may talk to your friends at the lunch table differently if your manager is sitting with you.

Brother Lawrence encourages us to purposefully change our mindset to focus on God, so that the dishes become no different than the aria.

It's not about, "Bless me. Bless me more. Give me stuff." It's about the pots and pans and things.

Why do we equate wealth and material goods with God's favor? Or, more likely, we assume that because we don't have something that someone else does, God is mad at us or disappointed or ignoring us altogether.

Make me a saint by getting meals.

(All hospital orderlies, stay-at-home parents, waiters and waitresses, cooks, and high school lunch ladies just sat a little taller.)

A saint by getting meals.

Saint: One separated from the world and consecrated to God; one holy by profession and by covenant.
—Easton's 1897 Bible Dictionary

Make me consecrated by the very Creator of ALL things by getting meals, mopping a floor, folding the laundry. Make me a saint by doing the most common of things.

It is possible to connect with God—soul to soul—by doing all the things you are already doing. Walking across campus, driving through rush hour, waiting in line at McDonald's.

That's what the practice of the presence is. Connecting. Staying connected.

Let's talk about the spiritual life.

03

A Monk's Disclaimer

I know that they are not many who reach this state; it is a grace which God bestows only on very few chosen souls, for this Unclouded Vision is a gift from His all-bounteous hand; yet, for the consolation of such as would fain embrace this holy practice, let me say that God seldom denies this gift to those who earnestly desire it; and if He do withhold this crowning mercy, be well assured that, by the practice of the Presence of God, with the aid of His all-sufficient grace, the soul can attain to a state, which approaches very nearly the Unclouded Vision. —Brother Lawrence

04

How to Live a Spiritual Life

Step 1: God Is Here: Stop Looking

That practice which is alike the most holy, the most general, and the most needful in the spiritual life is the practice of the Presence of God. *It is* the schooling of the soul to find its joy in His Divine Companionship, *holding with Him at all times and at every moment humble and loving converse, without set rule or stated method, in all time of our temptation and tribulation, in all time of our dryness of soul and disrelish of God, yes, and even when we fall into unfaithfulness and actual sin.* —Brother Lawrence

You would be surprised at how many people skip this basic step on their way to living a life that is spiritual. They get caught up in the why, where, and how of the spiritual life. They get so busy looking for God that they fail to understand that God is already here.

Picture a man gathering his things for a day at the pool. He has his towel, suntan lotion with the proper SPF, an iPod, flip-flops, and something from the summer reading list at Borders. He arrives at the pool, and, after carefully placing the goggles on his face and the swim fins on his feet, he dives into the pool and begins frantically searching. He takes a deep breath and excitedly pushes himself to the bottom, searching. When his lungs can no longer take it, he surfaces. He takes another gulp and throws himself down, this time following the sides of the pool. After a few minutes, others at the pool notice his behavior and come over to watch. They comment to each other, guessing the man has lost his car keys or perhaps his wife's prize ring. When the man can't swim anymore, he kicks to the top and quietly paddles to the side where he rests his head on the side of the pool, feeling the cool tiles on the skin of his forehead.

An older man wanders over as our swimmer pulls himself from the water. "What'd you lose there, sonny?"

"Nothing," the younger says. "I didn't lose anything."

"Well, what were you all fired up and looking for then?"

Pulling himself to his feet, the swimmer walks dejectedly to his chair and gathers his belongings. "Water," he says. "I was looking for water."

We don't have to search for God. God is surrounding us, drenching us to the bone with His presence. Once we understand that, we can work on how to make ourselves aware of it always. God is here in our best moments and our worst moments. God is here in the seasons of our year and the seasons of our lives.

God is here when we are sick, when we are tempted to do wrong, and when we act on those temptations. God is here when we doubt Him, deny Him, and ignore Him.

Understanding that God is present is not the same thing as understanding the presence. Let's move on.

Step 2: Conversation Not Recitation

We should apply ourselves unceasingly to this one end, to so rule all our actions that they be little acts of communion with God; but they must not be studied, they must come naturally, from the purity and simplicity of the heart.
—Brother Lawrence

Picture yourself as a small child on Thanksgiving. The parades are over, and now we are at grandma's house. The family is sitting around the table. The "good" china is out on the "good" tablecloth. The decorations in the center only come out of the closet at this time of year and are placed with much precision. They are so delicate that we (who must sit on telephone books to see) are not allowed to touch them. The table is covered with foods that took hours to prepare, and the room now smells like a thousand different flavors and spices. We bow our heads, fold our hands (or perhaps hold those on either side of us), and grandpa asks the blessing.

Or perhaps our first experience with prayer is in church, where we must sit and look at stained-glass windows and listen to the organ. The robed minister goes through the ritual and sacred utterances. We watch as those around us kneel or simply bow their heads as the minister prays, and we respond with recited lines. We are shushed if we make any noise or try to doodle on the back of an offering envelope.

This is prayer. Make no mistake … this is prayer. By praying this way, we show God we respect Him. We teach children about the sacredness of words and liturgy.

But this is not all that prayer is. Many of us don't even think about prayer until suppertime each evening or simply on Sunday morning. Brother Lawrence prayed while he did the dishes. We think of monks in their long robes and their sacred places. We think of the practiced chants. Praying while doing the dishes? What is he talking about? Heck, I do dishes. How is that a sacred thing?

The Scriptures tell us to "pray without ceasing" (1 Thess. 5:17, NKJV). Brother Lawrence understood this. He prayed in his kitchen and in his sanctuary. We can talk to the Creator of the universe while we drive our kids to football games, pack their lunches, fold the towels, and brush our teeth. By simply talking to God, rather than at God, we can turn prayer into a conversation.

"Oh wonderful Creator, as I, Your humble servant, doth fold these socks of the children You have blessed me with in Your divine mercy ..." vs in 2 Samuel 24?

I don't think that's what the good monk had in mind.

Talk to God like you would talk to a friend. Tell Him what is in your heart, what you're feeling, thinking, wondering—even if it is nothing at all or nothing you think is important enough to take to "the Almighty."

By all means, pray in the sanctuary. Pray around the Thanksgiving table. Pray in song and dance, in art and architecture. But also pray in your simplest moments. You have a lot more simple moments than you do Thanksgiving dinners. Pray without ceasing. God is listening. By praying all the time, you open your heart to God and will be able to hear His words and feel His presence all around you. As Bathsheba's son once did, ...?

Step 3: Careful and Constant

We must do all things thoughtfully and soberly without impetuosity or precipitancy, which denotes a mind undisciplined. We must go about our labors quietly, calmly, and lovely, entreating Him to prosper the works of our hands. —Brother Lawrence

Most of us are perfectly willing to invite Jesus to come and live in our hearts, but how many of us would be willing to invite Him into the minivan?

Chef Emeril Lagasse has taught us, "Cooking is about recipes. Baking is about formula." One thing I share with Brother Lawrence is the kitchen. I like to make meatloaf, lasagna, and pizzas. These are things I can play with, experimenting with flavors and ingredients. Add a half cup of chili-cheese dip to a meatloaf, and it won't matter one way or another. Leave the smallest ingredient out of chocolate-chip cookie batter (one-half teaspoon of baking powder), and see what kind of cookies you get.

Living a spiritual life is closer to baking. We must do things with great care and not throw in an extra cup of butterscotch chips on a whim. There are details of our lives we cannot leave out. Our children, our spouses, our own well-beings must be taken care of.

If we drive a vanload of kids to band practice, we don't drive up over the curb or across lawns. We should not talk on the cell phone, sign the permission slip, change the CD, and read a magazine about dental health all at the same time.

When we drive, we should drive, taking great care that we know what's riding in the seat behind us. When we live a spiritual life, we must take great care because we know that what we do is for God. God does not require us to bake seven-layer cakes with butter-cream frosting perfectly swirled into intricate patterns. God asks us to pay attention and give the same love to slicing the dough off the premade store-bought roll as we would to preparing a wedding cake from scratch.

We seldom give any attention to the details of living a spiritual life. Because we are "Christian" and believe in the omnipresent, omnipotent God, we think that these things will take care of themselves. Brother Lawrence found he felt closest to the Creator in his kitchen, doing mundane tasks. If we believe that God is in all things, as the Scriptures tell us, then God is present when we wash the dishes. God is present when we make a cheese sandwich. God is present when we fold the socks.

Step 4: In the Quiet

What offering is there more acceptable to God than thus throughout the day to quit the things of outward sense, and to withdraw to worship Him within the secret places of the soul? I am confident, it is a common error among religious persons, to neglect this practice of ceasing for a time that, which they are engaged upon, to worship God in the depth of their soul, and to enjoy the peace of brief communion with Him. —Brother Lawrence

Our society has realized the benefits of the weekend. (Except for a few overzealous teachers who just love to assign weekend homework or bosses who want the report on their desk Monday morning.) We also need our vacations. We ask about "time off" when we interview for a position, so we should take the same interest in "time off" from the chaos of life.

To acquire the spiritual life that Brother Lawrence is talking about, we must be willing to take a mental-spiritual vacation every chance we get. To make God a part of our everyday life, we must be willing to give God room every day. It sounds so simple, but even those who consider themselves to be Spirit-filled are often too busy to take a moment to be filled with the Spirit.

We must be willing to put aside the forms, the letters, the bills, the schedule, the television, and the computer and take a quiet moment to recognize whom we are dealing with. Take the time to be alone. Close the bedroom door for a minute or two. Step out of the chaotic kitchen and into the cool, dark garage. Take a moment in the quiet, even if it is in your car in the parking lot. Shut off the radio, quiet yourself, and say thank you. Recognize God for who He is. Invite Him into your heart. Ask Him to fulfill your needs. Thank Him for the blessings that He has given you. These mini-retreats, these temporary vacations alone keep us from being selfish. Selfishness can only exist in the real world. It dries up and blows away when we are with God.

This is not something we can do once and then forget. It is a "practice," a routine action performed until we don't have to remember to do it. Prayer does not need to take an hour. It does not need to be led by a clergy. A few minutes of quiet, open-hearted prayer done as many times a day as we can will open us more and more to the realization that we are constantly in the presence of pure love.

Step 5: Understand That You Can't Understand

We must unfeignedly believe that God is in very fact within our souls, and that we must worship Him and love Him and serve Him in spirit and in truth; that He sees all, and that unto Him all hearts are open, our own and those of all His creatures; that He is self-existent, whilst it is in Him that all His creatures live and move and have their being; that His Perfection is Infinite and Sovereign, and demands the full surrender of ourselves, our souls and bodies. In simple justice we owe Him all our thoughts and words and actions. Let us see to it that we pay our debt.
—Brother Lawrence

There is a bit of a trick here. Yes, we must recognize that God is all around us everywhere we go. Yes, we should speak with God like we are having a conversation. But we cannot, under any circumstances, forget exactly with whom we are dealing.

In the Walt Disney Company there is a team of creative thinkers who do nothing but think up the stuff that goes into the theme parks. They are called "concept designers." They sit in a room with walls made of cork, dry-erase boards, and paper. They fill the table with paints, markers, and crayons, and they decide what will be the next magic thing to put in the Magic Kingdom. Literally everything you would see as you walk through the streets of a Disney theme park came from the minds of the people sitting around a table with nothing on the schedule for the day except to think this stuff up.

When we speak of God, we are talking about the Creator of the very universe. We are talking about a being so far beyond our understanding that Walt Disney's best team of imagineers could not, on their best day, hope to come close to even one-billionth of what God is.

If we sit and ponder the idea that the ant ...
that sits on the leaf ...
of the tree ...
by the river ...
in the country ...
on the continent ...
by the ocean ...
that surrounds the planet ...
that rides in the solar system ...
on the outer spiral arm of the galaxy ...

All came from the imagination of one Being!

Our five senses and our three dimensions limit any thought we have about God. We cannot think beyond those. But God is limitless. He has limitless senses and limitless dimensions. How can we possibly understand all that God is?

As we begin to conceptualize that, we must also realize that there is so much MORE! When we pray, it is to *that* God. When we sing, it is *that* God we are singing about.

One of the greatest gifts God gave us is that we don't have to understand Creator God in order to love Creator God. Once we grasp that understanding God is not a prerequisite to feeling His presence, we can overcome one of the greatest roadblocks to our goal.

Step 6: Self-Examination

Necessity is laid upon us to examine ourselves with diligence to find out what are the virtues, which we chiefly lack, and which are the hardest for us to acquire; we should seek to learn the sins that do most easily beset us, and the times and occasions, when we do most often fall. In the time of struggle we ought to have recourse to God with perfect confidence, abiding steadfast in the Presence of His Divine Majesty; in lowly adoration we should tell out before Him our griefs and our failures, asking Him lovingly for the succor of His grace; and in our weakness we shall find in Him our strength. —Brother Lawrence

Let's say you live in Cleveland, Ohio. It is February. Cleveland is a wonderful town, but it has been said that God invented February in Cleveland so that people who don't drink could know what a hangover is like. You decide that this would be a good time to visit your relatives in Florida. Perhaps you'll rent a beach chair and let the ocean waters come up as you bury your feet in the warm sand. You pack a bag, pick up interstate 71 and find US-1. Now there are a mere eighteen hours between you and the Welcome to Florida rest stop in Jacksonville.

Between here and there you will find every imaginable attraction off to the side of the road. Just a few miles off any exit, you will find homemade fudge, live nude girls, pecans, antiques, five-for-$10 T-shirts, motels, hotels, giant plaster dinosaur museums, genuine Southern cooking, monuments to every political figure ever born, and more live nude girls.

If you don't make it to your spot in the beach, whose fault is that?

If we are going to live this spiritual life, we have to be willing to take a good honest look at our shortcomings. We need to stay out of places where we know we will be tempted and keep our eyes on the road no matter what the billboards offer us just a few miles off the next exit. Once we can honestly say, "This is where I fall short. This is where I'm lacking. This is where I screw up," then we can go to God. God will not turn us away in disappointment. God will welcome us. God will see our hearts and give us comfort, strength, and courage.

The means to acquiring a spiritual life have nothing to

do with giving up the things you love, being someone you are not, memorizing the Bible till you can quote it for any occasion. Acquiring a spiritual life is about recognizing God, making time for God, admitting our shortcomings to God, and understanding that God is here.

You will not achieve all of these tomorrow. The fifth-grader who just picked up the trombone is not going to play Carnegie Hall next week. The practice of the presence of God is closer to, say, the "practice" of a doctor. This is my practice. This is what I do. The more we do it, the more we can lead a spiritual life.

05

How to Love God

It is amazing how complicated we make things in the name of religion. As soon as we start making lists of dos and don'ts, we get ourselves in trouble. Brother Lawrence wrote three simple ideas for loving the Creator. He called these "Of how it is required of us to worship God in spirit and in truth."

Step 1: Love God with All That You Are

To worship God in spirit and in truth means to offer to Him the worship that we owe. God is a Spirit; therefore we must worship Him in spirit and in truth,—that is to say, by presenting to Him a true and humble spiritual worship in the very depth of our being. God alone can see this worship, which, offered unceasingly, will in the end become as it were natural, and as if He were one with our soul, and our soul one with Him: practice will make this clear.
—Brother Lawrence

God is not your waiter. God is not Santa. God is not your buddy. Whatever we give to God, we give it because we owe it to Him. Understand that. We owe God. Not the other way around. There is nothing that we are *owed* by God. God gave you life. Start there. You are walking around on this planet because God started things in motion. God was responsible for creating the universe, and God was responsible for your parents going out on that first date. God was there when you were born.

Psalm 139—We Are God's (author's paraphrase)

> God, you know me.
> God, you know me.
> Better than my parents know me.
> Better than my friends know me.
> Better than I know myself.
> You knew me before I was born.
> You knew me before the universe was born.
> There is no place that I can be without you.
> If I were to climb the highest of mountains,
> You would be there.
> If I could breathe underwater and swam to
> the bottom of the sea,
> You would be there.
> If I could grow wings like the angels and soar
> to the heavens,
> You would be there waiting for me.
> I can't begin to know all that you are.
> Your thoughts are beyond my comprehension
> to understand.

God, you know me.
You know there are those around me who
don't follow your ways.
They think I am a fool.
Protect me, God.
Keep me close to you.
Amen.

God created us. We must say "thank you." The Bible
tells us that all good things come from God. Below is a
partial list ...

Trees, rain, snow, hot fudge sauce, Chuck Taylor
high-top tennis shoes, Ben & Jerry's, peanut butter,
bus drivers, ambulance drivers, garbage collectors,
candles that smell like the ocean, books, CDs, *The
Simpsons*, Starbucks, matches, sleeping bags, stars,
planets, rockets, telescopes, movies, DVDs, warm
socks, warm hands, warm hearts, family, vacations,
vacations with the family, vacations without the
family, the Grand Canyon, rest stops, public toilets,
indoor plumbing, agriculture, corn, peas, lettuce,
carrots, hot jalapeno peppers, pizza, cheese, cows,
chocolate milk, Oreo cookies, plastic bags to put
your lunch in, metal lunch boxes, thermoses, cool
mountain streams, the smell of pine needles in the
woods, the smell of pine needles in your living room,
Christmas, Easter, vaccinations, vitamins, laughter,
giggles, smirks, grins, smiles, laughter through tears,
tears through laughter, jokes that make you squirt
milk out of your nose, and onions.

Say "thank you."

This is not just a "thank you" the way you say "thank you" to your grandmother who still gives you PJs because she has labored under the delusion that you have been eight for the last fifteen years. This is a "thank you" from down in the depths of your soul. This is a "thank you" that is a realization that all good things come from God. Everything you take for granted. Everything you never thought of. Everything.

This is a "thank you" that should be shouted from a mountaintop. This is a "thank you" that should be heard from your driveway when you walk out in the rain to get the paper in the morning. This is a "thank you" that comes from the heart. Say "thank you" with your life.

The best way to say "thank you" to God is by taking the gifts He has given you and giving them back to Him. If God has given you the gift of being able to sing, sing for God. Volunteer to do a solo on Christmas Eve.

If you have a God-given gift to cook, cook for God. There's a shelter in your neighborhood. Or maybe you can cook for your church youth group some night. If you can organize and straighten better than anyone you know, organize and straighten for God. Your church has a craft closet that's a living nightmare.

God gives everyone gifts. All good things come from God. Say "thank you."

Step 2: Recognize That God Is God

To worship God in truth is to acknowledge Him to be what He is, and ourselves as what in very fact we are. To worship Him in truth is to acknowledge with heart-felt sincerity what God in truth is,—that is to say, infinitely perfect, worthy of infinite adoration, infinitely removed from sin, and so of all the Divine attributes. That man is little guided by reason, who does not employ all his powers to render to this great God the worship that is His due.
—Brother Lawrence

Let's start with the Psalms again.

Psalm 84—Turn It Up! (author's paraphrase)

> I want you to relax. You are in the house of
> the Lord.
> We will turn it up.
> Play it loud.
> The Spirit of God is here, now. *+ in INVICT....*
> There is a Spirit here tonight that cannot be
> ignored.
> Everyone sing.
> Dance.
> We are the children of the Creator of the
> universe.
> God is the sunrise after a dark night.
> God is the rain on dry grass.
> God is the answer to our prayer.
> One day in the presence of God is better than
> a thousand years alone. *of with parents or kids?*

41

We are in the house of God.
God is all-powerful.
God will stay with us.
Forever.
Amen.

Walt Disney himself was said to be one of the most creative people on the planet, and a lot of his ideas for the Disney theme parks are only now becoming reality because the technology at the time could not keep up with his ideas.

Henry Ford had one wall of his office painted white and kept free of art or furniture. He would sit in his office and visualize ideas on that wall as if it were a movie screen.

Thomas Edison had a summer home in Florida. Off to the side of the house was a small cottage that held a dining room and a kitchen. Every once in a while he would invite Henry Ford, Harvey Firestone, and some other guest, who they thought would be a creative thinker, over. They would have dinner in that little cottage and just brainstorm ideas about where the world would be in a hundred years.

If you put Albert Einstein, Walt Disney, Thomas Edison, Henry Ford, Stephen Hawking, and Gene Roddenberry around one table ... all of them ... together ... on their best day ... they could not even come close to the awesome creative power of God.

As I mentioned in chapter 4, I love my kitchen, and it's a great feeling for me to have four burners, the oven, and the microwave all going at the same time. When all the food gets done at the same time, I'm feeling pretty darn good about myself. Imagine doing that with a planet. Imagine doing that with a universe.

Now, imagine doing that for a house full of company. It's Christmastime, and everyone from your office and your spouse's office is in your home. What would it be like to have half the room eat without a "thank you" or a compliment? What would it be like to have a significant portion of those in attendance say out loud that you didn't do the cooking at all? It's a good thing that I am not God.

Step 3: Recognize That You Are Not God

Furthermore, to worship God in truth is to confess that we live our lives entirely contrary to His will, and contrary to our knowledge that, were we but willing, He would fain make us conformable to Him. Who will be guilty of such folly as to withhold even for a moment the reverence and the love, the service and the unceasing worship that we owe to Him? —Brother Lawrence were designed to

Perhaps this will be clearer if we look at the book of Job. Remember Job? One of the earliest mentions of Satan in the Bible is of a wager between God and Satan. Satan is referred to here as one of God's "sons." They make a bet to see if Job will renounce God if God takes back all his blessings. God takes away everything Job has—his land, his livestock, and all his sons and daughters. Job gets beaten down, and when he can't take it any longer, he launches into a rant that spans several chapters. God then sits the boy down and lays it out for him. *bring back kids?*

who cares what delusional Satan thinks?

Where were you when I laid the earth's foundation? Tell me, if you understand. Who marked off its dimensions? Surely you know! Who stretched a measuring line across it? On what were its footings set, or who laid its cornerstone—while the morning stars sang together and all the angels shouted for joy?

Who shut up the sea behind doors when it burst forth from the womb, when I made the clouds its garment and wrapped it in thick darkness, when I fixed limits for it and set its doors and bars in place, when I said, "This far you may come and no farther; here is where your proud waves halt"?

Have you ever given orders to the morning, or shown the dawn its place, that it might take the earth by the edges and shake the wicked out of it? The earth takes shape like clay under a seal; its features stand out like those of a garment. The wicked are denied their light, and their upraised arm is broken.

Have you journeyed to the springs of the sea or walked in the recesses of the deep? Have

05

the gates of death been shown to you? Have
you seen the gates of the shadow of death?
Have you comprehended the vast expanses of
the earth? Tell me, if you know all this. (Job
38:4-18)

It goes on and on ... it's a great speech. It's also one of
those places in the Bible where it sounds like God has
a sense of humor. Read it again with sarcastic tone and
see if it doesn't sound a little humorous. God is the
sarcastic parent saying, "Do I look stupid?" or "Do you
think I'm made of money?" God knows what Job does
not—that He's going to give Job everything back. He's
going to bless Job like he's never been blessed before,
but first they're going to have this little heart-to-heart
or rather fed-up-man-to-raging-storm conversation.

One of the hardest things for us to get through our
heads is that we are not God. We don't get to make
the decisions. We don't get to decide what is and what
isn't. We have some power, but not complete power
over nature. Every time we start to push the limits of
God, He gives us a little reminder. Does the phrase
"even God couldn't sink this ship" ring any bells?

We are not God. Brother Lawrence tells us that this
is one of the steps to recognize if we are going to fully
love God.

We get mad at God because grandma died. We get
mad at God because we didn't get the girl/boy we
were after. We get mad at God because we lost a job.

We get mad at God because He didn't answer our prayer for that new car.

In order to fully experience the presence of God, we have to get over the fact that God is God and we are not.

When we get down life's road a little more, we often find out what God had in mind. We didn't get that job we wanted and then found a better one six months down the road. We finally realized how much pain grandma was in, and it wasn't God who made her suffer—it was God who let her suffering end. And if we really want to stand on the mountaintop and scream at God because of the car, we might want to sit down and re-evaluate our priorities.

06

Starting This Journey

In the coming chapters we will explore exactly what this "presence" is. We will talk about living a spiritual life and how a "union of the soul" with God is possible.

But we have to start somewhere ... So we will start here.

This isn't easy. It never was. You have chosen a path filled with many challenges. This life you have chosen to live can be hard. This God you have chosen to follow is sometimes hard to hear.

There are certain things you must know before undertaking any job. If you are going to make furniture, it's a good idea to know how the tools work. If you are going to cook, you should know that eggs make things rise. These are simple things to anyone with experience, but basic concepts that must be understood before going further. Brother Lawrence wrote down these basic principles, and they serve as a launching pad—a primer, if you will—for the rest of his teachings.

God in All Things

We must study ever to regard God and His Glory in all that we do, and say, and undertake. This is the end *that we should set before ourselves, to offer to God a sacrifice of perfect worship in this life, as we hope to do through all eternity. We ought firmly to resolve to overcome, with the grace of God assisting us, the many difficulties which will meet us in the spiritual life.* —Brother Lawrence

God is in all things. Got that? God is in the smell of the coffee that rests in my cup a few inches to the right of my computer. God is in my computer. God is in the wind that's blowing the grass outside of my window. God is in the grass. God is in the window. God is in the sunshine. God is in the plastic Jesus nightlight that is plugged into my wall. (It was a gift.) God is in all things. Not just the pretty things and not just the things that we believe are good and moral and true. God is in all things.

We must try to live so that everything we do is for God. In every action, let us think about God. Let us wonder about God. Let us be totally aware of God's presence in every moment of our lives.

You can't snap your fingers and live like this right

now. You just can't. And you cannot give up and put this book down because you can't live like this just yet. This is process. This is a series of lessons that must be learned and relearned. You may make every effort to connect your soul with God and feel nothing. Eventually you will. Eventually you will feel a change inside you. Others may even see a change in you. You will learn to be comfortable in your own skin.

read bits of Bible, but not every bit

When we die, the skin is not necessary. All the other physical limitations that keep us from God will do so no longer, and we may make the connection permanent. For now we do the best that we can.

Have you ever seen a piece of bailing twine? It wraps hay bails and (in the old days) packages. Study a piece of bailing twine, and you see that it is not one piece at all, but thousands of pieces wrapped around each other. One piece is easily broken ... and two ... and three, but eventually you will reach the point where you cannot break the string on your own. *schisms*

a bit more chapter

Connecting to the presence works like this. When we begin, it will be as though one tiny strand connects us to the soul of God. A slight movement, a veering thought, and the connection breaks. The longer you practice the presence, the more strands you connect to God until breaking the connection is not an option.

Once you start practicing the presence, you have to make up your mind that you are going to stick with it. It's like a diet. One month goes by and you've done well, but then you start to think, "Well, one pizza with extra cheese isn't going to hurt, is it? Just one sausage McMuffin ... that's all. I've been good. I haven't had one in months ... Just this once, and I'll skip half my lunch." Eventually we are saying, "Yeah, I was on a diet. I need to get back on it again."

Life is full of obstacles—spiritual obstacles, emotional obstacles, and mental obstacles. It is by the grace of God that we get over, around, under, or through them.

Wait a minute. I have two hands, a strong will, a sense of determination, and intelligence, and all of these combined got me through my problems, right? Yes. All those plus God.

God is with you. God is in you. God is around you. What you accomplish is by God's good grace. He gave you the hands, the will, the determination, and He was in your soul guiding you whether you were aware of it or not. Understand this. God is in all things.

A Mirror to the Soul

When we enter upon the spiritual life, we ought to consider thoroughly what we are, probing to the very depth. We shall find that we are altogether deserving of contempt, unworthy of the name of Christ, prone to all manner of maladies and subject to countless infirmities, which distress us and impair the soul's health, rendering us wavering and unstable in our humors and dispositions; in fact, creatures whom it is God's will to chasten and make humble by numberless afflictions and adversities, as well within as without. —Brother Lawrence

We are going to have to take a good long look at ourselves. Before we can begin, we have to look in a sort of "soul mirror" and see ourselves for what we are.

This is not to say we have to be perfect. This means we have to be aware that we are not perfect. Maybe you have a little problem with ego, pride, forgiveness, self-esteem, anger, or whatever else other books say you can fix by putting it all in Jesus' hands. Brother Lawrence said, "You're not perfect. Deal with that."

Ignoring a problem doesn't make it go away. Holding up a mirror to the soul simply means that we must recognize those problem places in our lives.

Look at them, "probing to the depth," and seek out those places where the warts and blemishes you spot in the reflection are keeping your soul from a connection.

Make an effort. If you look in the soul mirror and spot conceit, then pray about that. Talk to God. Consciously make an effort to listen rather than talk, to see issues from other viewpoints, to spend less time fighting for your way and more time trying to find a solution.

When we connect to God with unhealthy souls, the connection cannot be stable. Remember those little toys you used to get in cereal boxes called Wacky Wall Walkers? Maybe you got them from the vending machine at Wal-Mart. They were basically odd-shaped creatures covered in some sort of goo. Throw one against a wall, and it would slowly "creep" its way down to the floor.

It was a great toy for about fifteen minutes. Then it got dusty or you tried to carry it around in your pocket, and it didn't stick so well anymore. Finally it didn't stick to the wall at all no matter how hard you threw it.

Our connection with God works this way. Sometimes our souls get dusty and impair that connection. Eventually we wind up hurling ourselves against the wall again and again until we get hurt or discouraged and we stop trying.

If we are going to make the practice of the presence our "employment," as Brother Lawrence said, if we are going to make this connection an important part of our lives, we must look in the soul mirror and find the places we need to be dusted off.

Time-Out

We must believe steadfastly, never once doubting, that such discipline is for our good, that it is God's will to visit us with chastening, that it is the course of His Divine Providence to permit our souls to pass through all manner of sore experiences and times of trial, and for the love of

God to undergo divers sorrows and afflictions for so long as shall seem needful to Him; since, without this submission of heart and spirit to the will of God, devotion and perfection cannot subsist. —Brother Lawrence

Ever get your rear smacked when you were a kid? Spend a lot of time-outs in the corner contemplating your thumbs?

Even though we acknowledge God as "Our Father who art in heaven" every Sunday morning, it is hard to accept Him as a loving parent who must discipline His children.

Lessons hurt sometimes.

Maybe once your mom said, "Don't touch that; it's hot." Did you find out the hard way that moms don't lie?

As you grew older, perhaps you hooked up with some loser, and all your friends and family offered advice to dump them, and you didn't, so you got burned again.

Lessons hurt sometimes.

The Bible tells us: "No discipline seems pleasant at the time, but painful. Later on, however, it produces a harvest of righteousness and peace for those who have been trained by it" (Heb. 12:11).

Sometimes God gives us a time-out. Sometimes God

wants us to know who exactly is in charge. Sometimes God allows us to hurt ourselves so that we learn what we need to learn in order to move on.

This does not make God a vengeful and vindictive God. This does not mean God is punishing you. This means that God is trying to teach you something, and the more you resist, the more it's going to hurt.

It's like those finger traps common at kids' birthday parties when you were little. Stick one of your fingers in each end, and you can't get them back out, no matter how hard you pull. It's only when you stop and relax and step back that you can ease your pinkies out of the toy.

Stop fighting it. Step back and look at the problem. Learn what you need to know. Pull your fingers out and move on.

07

What Is the Presence?

The Presence of God is an applying of our spirit to God, or a realization of God as present, which is borne home to us either by the imagination or by the understanding.
—Brother Lawrence

God is present all the time, and all the time God is present. We can experience the presence when we simply pick up a book and learn about God. Right now you are experiencing the presence of God. You have chosen to learn. You have chosen to find a way to make the connection. That, in and of itself, connects you to God.

You can experience God in your dreams. The Bible is full of people who connected with the divine while they were sleeping. Joseph had dreams of his future. God showed him what his life was going to be and then put him through hell to get him ready for it.

You can simply sit quiet and meditate on God, and He will become present to you. Yes, this is hard to describe. Several times Brother Lawrence attempted to write down what the presence was, only to tear the paper up later because he felt the words he had written didn't come close to what he had experienced.

In the excerpt below, Brother Lawrence talks at length about a friend whom he had known for forty years. Whether this friend was another monk or someone who Brother Lawrence taught the "practice" to is unclear from his writings. But he was impressed enough by his friend to talk about the ways his friend had achieved the "presence" and how he referred to it.

> A simple *act*
> A clear and distinct *knowledge* of God
> A *view* as through a glass
> A loving *gaze*
> An inward sense of God
> A *waiting* on God
> A silent *converse* with Him
> A *repose* in Him
> The *life* and *peace* of the soul

The Connection of the Soul

Brother Lawrence wrote that "there are three degrees of union of the soul with God."

1. The General Union: This is the connection that occurs because we are children of God. You don't have to be aware of it. You don't have to believe it. You don't even have to be a Christian. By this rule, even atheists have a connection to God because they are His children. I have this connection. You have this connection. Osama Bin Laden has this connection. The kid who can never get my order straight at McDonald's has this connection, and so does the mother on her cell phone in the SUV who cut me off as I drove the carpool to school this morning. We are all connected at this level.

2. The Virtual Union: The word "virtual" is misleading here. It has nothing to do with computers or virtual reality. The virtual union, as Brother Lawrence wrote, is more like a practical union or an effective union. This is something we have all experienced whether we are aware of it or not. It is the emotion that comes when our soul is temporarily closer to God.

If you have ever been to a concert, you know that there is a moment at the end, a moment of euphoria, when you feel a buzz even though you haven't been drinking. No drugs. No alcohol. This is pure euphoria that goes beyond the adrenaline rush. It's as if you are connected to the souls of every other person in the room. The crowd stands as one, lighters in the air, as the band finishes out the last tune of the evening.

You may have felt this practical union in church. Perhaps on Christmas Eve, when the sermon is done, and the choir is singing "Silent Night," and everyone holds candles. In college I was a summer camp counselor, and I enjoyed the quiet mornings before campers arrived for the week. I would get up early and take my coffee down to the balcony of the lodge and watch the sun come up.

You might get this feeling when you drive. When the sun is just right, the temperature is perfect, and you roll down your window and turn up the radio, it becomes a perfect moment. Perhaps an oldies song does it for you as you cruise along by the shore. Maybe you prefer some Celtic hymn as you drive through a wooden glade and the sunshine pours through the leaves.

Virtual union is that right-place-right-time moment. Life can be full of these.

3. The Actual Union: The perfect union of the soul with God is a continuous feeling. Unlike the other unions where it can feel like the soul is in a meditative state, in the actual union the soul is alive ... intensely alive. Brother Lawrence said the soul in the actual union state is "quicker than fire and more luminous than the sun." This is not a fleeting emotion. It does not blaze and then burn out. Instead of a state of mind, think of this as a state of soul. Deeply spiritual yet very simple. It fills us with a joy that is calm, a love that is reverent. This state lifts the soul to new heights.

Where the sense of the love of God constrains it to adore Him, and to embrace Him with a tenderness that cannot be expressed, and which experience alone can teach us to understand. —Brother Lawrence

Not everything that is good for the body is good
for the soul. Great music, astounding artwork,
Krispy Kreme donuts, the smell of coffee, the lights
on your Christmas tree when you are not wearing
your glasses—these things may act as doorways
to the presence, but the presence itself may have
to be reached after putting aside these "worldly"
things. The presence itself is a detachment of all the
things on earth and a union with God. This can be
experienced only through love. Things of sight and
sound and smell will have limits because they are part
of our humanity. As humans we are naturally limited.
Worldly things may launch us where we need to go,
but they will eventually reach a stopping point. They
can only take us so far. Love will take us further to
where the only logical end is God.

If we just think about God, if we ponder, wonder,
consider, contemplate, muse, and mull over all that
we believe about God, if we do this with purposeful
repetition, eventually it will become habit.

Years ago I went to college with a guy who had a part-
time job in the cafeteria. He worked in the dish room.
In the dining hall students could place their trays of
dirty dishes on a conveyer belt. The belt would take
the tray back into the dish room, where my friend
would scrape the remaining food into a small trough
where the food would be washed into a disposal.
He would rinse the plates, put cups and glasses in
a special rack, stack the silverware in a container
according to type, and then send all of this down the

line to someone else who would put them into the dishwasher.

It was hot, sweltering work, and he spent much of that school year in a sort of fast because when he looked at the remains of other people's food, he lost much of his appetite. He eventually got to a point where the work was so routine that he could do it without thinking. He set his body on "automatic pilot" and allowed his mind to drift away. He thought about girls, home, school, girls, how he would make his car payment, how he would explain his grades to his parents, and more girls. He was in the dish room of the cafeteria, but his mind was thousands of miles away.

Brother Lawrence told us that we can experience the presence of God this way: We can be in our bodies, but we can allow our souls to drift upward and connect with God on an intimate level. And we can teach ourselves to do this without thinking.

Last year near Christmastime as my church was preparing for the children's Christmas pageant, a young single mother in our church came up to me with her three-year-old son and handed me the child's necktie. She said, "I have no idea how to work one of these things." I smiled and took the young man by the hand, and we stepped off to the side. Suddenly I realized that neither did I. I have been able to tie my necktie since I was about eight, but with this three-year-old in front of me, I was stumped. I actually had to turn the little guy around and stand behind him to get him looking spiffy for his concert.

I never *think* about how to tie a tie. I simply tie a tie.

According to Brother Lawrence, this purposeful dwelling on God will make it habit. We do not have to remind ourselves to breathe in or out. Neither should we have to remind ourselves that God is in this world, that God is in our hearts, that God is closer to us than our own skin.

The Reason They Call It "Practice"

I did not learn to tie my necktie the first time I tried. I learned after many times of practicing. Then after many times, I still had to watch myself in the mirror. It is only now that I can tie my necktie without thinking.

When I first bought a new remote for my television, it took me a week to figure out the buttons, which one would turn off the set and which one would record my favorite shows.

To Brother Lawrence this connection, the "actual union," occurs at the very depth of one's being. This is the place where the soul speaks to God. In fact Brother Lawrence talked about this as if he had no conscious awareness of what was going on between the soul and God.

When this connection happens, the rest of the world is blotted out. Brother Lawrence described this as if the outside world were no more than "a fire of straw."

Let us mark well, however, that this intercourse with God he holds in the depth of his being; *there it is that the soul speaks to God, heart to heart, and over the soul thus holding converse there steals a great and profound peace.*
—Brother Lawrence

Everything temporal passes without concern to the soul—like a piece of straw quickly consumed by fire. How amazing would it be to think that the job, the school, the car payments, the relationship, the office, the boss burn bright for a moment and don't distract us from what we are doing.

Brother Lawrence also believed that this connection, which occurs down deep in the soul, shows on the outside. Have you ever known someone who seemed to have all the reasons in the world not to be happy, yet somehow he or she still was?

Bud was an amazing older man in my church. He was constantly telling jokes or stories that would make you laugh. It wasn't that he was always happy, because he wasn't. Instead, he always seemed at peace with himself. He was comfortable in his own skin. He was making jokes right up until the hours before he died.

God likes meeting the soul.

Great would be our surprise, if we but knew what converse the soul holds at these times with God, who seems to

so delight in this communion, that to the soul, which would fain abide ever with Him, He bestows favors past numbering; and as if He dreaded lest the soul should turn again to things of earth, He provides for it abundantly, so that the soul finds in faith a nourishment divine, a joy that has no measure, beyond its utmost thought and desire; and this without a single effort on its part but simple consent.
—Brother Lawrence

God:	Hey, I've got a present for you.
Us:	What's the catch?
God:	There's no catch. It's just a gift.
Us:	What is it?
God:	Peace of mind. Rest of soul. Joy beyond your comprehension.
Us:	Is that like a book?
God:	No. It's a communion with Me.
Us:	I take communion in church.
God:	This is different.
Us:	Do I have to sign something?
God:	No, I can just give this to you, and it will make you feel good.
Us:	It's like drugs? I don't do drugs.
God:	It's not drugs.
Us:	What is it then?
God:	It's not tangible. It's more like a feeling.
Us:	Can I see it?
God:	No, I just said it isn't tangible.
Us:	Hear it? Smell it? Taste it? Touch it?
God:	No ... it's not like that.
Us:	Then how can You sell it to me?

God:	It's not for sale. It's a gift.
Us:	Why do You want to give me a gift?
God:	Because I love you.
Us:	If You love me, why don't You just give it to me? Why do You make me ask for it? That's kind of controlling, isn't it?
God:	I'm not keeping it from you. You just have to accept it.
Us:	Why do You always have these rules?
God:	Never mind.

The presence of God is right in front of us. It's there all the time because God is there all the time. Any roadblocks that stand in the way of our experiencing the presence are of our own creation.

A few years back, a company came out with a series of small porcelain statues of Jesus helping His little ones on earth play sports. Maybe you have seen these: One statue depicted Jesus as a sort of referee while two small uniformed children played basketball. The problem was that the statue looked like Jesus was holding the ball above their little heads where they couldn't get to it, as if the Son of God was playing some sort of Holy Keep-Away.

God doesn't work this way. All His love, all His gifts, all His blessings are right in front of us. We don't have to ask. We don't have to beg. We don't have to recite some secret words in order to receive them. We just have to reach out and take them.

So then the question becomes "how?" How do we receive this gift ? How do we open ourselves up for the presence of the Creator of the universe?

08

How to Acquire the Presence

The Presence of God is thus the life and nourishment of the soul, *and with the aid of His grace, it can attain thereunto by diligent use of the means I will now set out.*
—Brother Lawrence

In his writings, Brother Lawrence defined what he believed were the steps for attaining the presence of God. These steps are deceptively simple. They require sacrifice. They require discipline. Much of the process of acquiring the presence of God is like running off the diving board to do a cannonball and at the last minute, chickening out. Once you start, you can't go back.

Step 1: Purity

The first is a great purity of life; in guarding ourselves with care lest we should do or say or think on anything, which might be displeasing to God. —Brother Lawrence

In my local newspaper, usually at the back of the Life & Times section, is a column called "The Ticked-Off Column." It's a quarter page of small snippets sent and called in by readers. They get a paragraph or so to vent frustrations about what's ticking them off this week. Often there are complaints about stores, fast-food restaurants, women who do their makeup while driving, standardized tests, SUVs, and cell phones. Sometimes there is one about people who drive SUVs while talking on cell phones and doing their makeup. It's a quarter page of complaining and moaning, and it's very popular. So popular in fact that one of the local radio stations has taken to reading the column aloud on the air every day, and then playing reruns of the segment on the weekends.

I used to read this column every day and then guess which complaints I'd hear on the radio a few hours later. I eventually came to the conclusion that when I listened to the ticked-off segment, I felt ugly inside. It wasn't funny. It was just listening to someone else complain. I stopped listening to that radio station and quit reading the column. Surprisingly, I started having much better mornings.

Now let's clarify. When we say "things that are displeasing to God," there's a tendency to hear the word "sin," and not just the word but to hear it with a pulpit pounding preacher's accent, "Sinnnnnnn" (visualize pointing finger now).

Sin is a separation from God. We get this word from

the same place we get the word Satan, which does not mean a little red guy with horns. Sin means "separation." Satan means "obstacle." Again we hear the preacher's voice saying that sin is smoking, drinking, sex, greed, and an ever-growing list of what would appear on most people's top ten list of fun things to do.

I know a minister who went to seminary in the South. The campus was built on donated land that used to be a tobacco field. The seminary was surrounded by tobacco fields, and the board, the professors, and most of the students smoked tobacco in one form or another. Yet they produced some amazing clergy. Can we point to this and say, "Sinnnnnnn"? I don't think so.

When Brother Lawrence wrote about guarding ourselves lest we should think or say anything that is displeasing to God, he wasn't necessarily talking about a list of behaviors that make certain Christians uncomfortable. We are taking about things that separate us from the Creator.

Step 2: Focus

The second is a great faithfulness in the practice of His Presence, *and in keeping the soul's gaze fixed on God in faith, calmly, humbly, lovingly, without allowing an entrance to anxious cares and disquietude.*
—Brother Lawrence

Disquietude is a very cool word. It means to have

feelings of anxiety or uneasiness that make you tense or irritable. Too often this is how we approach God. Ken Davis, a noted speaker, often says, "There isn't a parent in this room who has not spent a Sunday morning with their hands around the throat of a child they love dearly."

Getting up and going to church becomes an ordeal. We sit in pews and think of the things we could be doing. We concentrate with intensity on ripping the check out of the checkbook one perforation at a time, hoping that no one will hear the cht...cht...cht........ cht-cht.

We notice the cobwebs in the lights. We notice the noise our stomachs make. We notice whose kids are brats. We notice that the choirmaster is drifting off and leaning slightly to port. We notice that there are exactly seven spelling or grammatical errors in the bulletin and wonder why they don't use spell check.

Part of the problem is that when we go to church, we think we are an audience. More and more churches are being built like theaters. There's a stage, a light show, a drop-down screen, and a sound system with a killer band. All the focus is on the stage. Pastors become actors and eventually stars.

If you travel outside of the United States, you find that the churches in other countries, by their very architecture, are designed to lift the face, lift the voice, and lift the spirit. The congregation is not an audience. The choir, the pastor, the people sitting in the pews, the band, the liturgist, or any other worship "helper" are all part of the same worship experience. God is the audience. The pastor and the congregation are on an equal tier. We are there to worship God ... together.

There are debates in every church across the country as to whether or not children should be welcomed in the worship service. The argument is that a squirming child is too distracting. Children squirm. That's their job. Especially if you put them in uncomfortable clothes and tell them to sit and be quiet. Exactly whom do children distract? God? Last time I checked, God loved kids.

I lost count of the number of my reports cards I brought home with "He's a smart boy, but he lacks focus" written in the teacher comments section. I've had a focus problem all of my life. Brother Lawrence taught that it is much more difficult to attain God's presence when we are beset by a disquietude.

You can say, "Sure, it was easy for Brother Lawrence. He didn't have to deal with children or other distractions. He was able to kneel in a monastery and be in the middle of a silent room."

True enough, but perhaps you too will experience God's presence when you are alone. Shut your door. Find a rooftop. Go sit in your car. God's not waiting for you to sit in a pew. He's waiting for you to listen.

Turn off the noise. Calm down. Get over yourself. Tell God you love Him and start there.

Step 3: Look to God

Make it your study, before taking up any task to look to God, be it only for a moment, as also when you are engaged thereon, and lastly when you have performed the same. As forasmuch as without time and great patience this practice cannot be attained, be not disheartened at your many falls; truly this habit can only be formed with difficulty, yet when it is so formed, how great will be your joy therein!
—Brother Lawrence

Love God. Start there. End there. Live there. God is the reason you are on this planet, and He is the reason you are reading this book. Tell Him so, without fanfare or waving your arms in the air. Tell God you love Him, that you want to know His presence all the time. When you wake up in the morning, thank God for the day. When you go to sleep at night, thank God for the day behind you and the night ahead. Thank God for sheets and pillows. Thank God for your spouse and the smell of her hair and the feel of her back pressed against your chest.

As you move through the day, be aware of God. Thank God for the teeth you are brushing. Thank God for the school you attend or the job you have to go to. When your boss yells, thank God for the paycheck. Say grace over your meals. If it's winter, feel the cold air as it enters the lungs that God gave you and thank

Him for the air. Think about the creativity involved in designing snowflakes. If it is summer, thank God for the warmth of the sun on your skin.

Are you getting the idea? Make God a part of your every day. Many people don't think about God until Sunday, and then they wonder: "God, where have You been? I've had such a crummy week." Then God is out of their life for another seven days. You don't have to recite a prayer before you switch the station on the car radio. But make yourself aware that God made music. You don't have to go into a lengthy theological dissertation before making a copy of the annual report, but remember that God is in charge of all things.

These little "flits" with God need only be a moment. But they must be a part of your life to attain the presence of God.

This is not easy. Do not get to the end of the day and think, "Well, I certainly didn't think about God enough today." It is a habit that must be formed over a long time. Over time you will remember to do it more. Over time you will do it by habit. Over time you will do it without thinking, and then it is taken over by your soul.

Step 4: Surrender

Those who set out upon this practice let me counsel to offer up in secret a few words, such as "My God, I am wholly Thine. O God of Love, I love Thee with all my heart. Lord, make my heart even as Thine"; or such other words as love prompts on the instant. But take heed that your mind wanders not back to the world again; keep it fixed on God alone, so that, thus subdued by the will, it may be constrained to abide with God. —Brother Lawrence

OK, maybe "God, I am wholly Thine" doesn't quite fit the bill anymore. Try this one ... "Speak, God, your servant is listening."

Just that much. Just six words. Find a quiet place or become aware that your world around you is giving you "space" and simply say, "Speak, God, your servant is listening."

Do not go to God in prayer with your wish list. God is not Santa Claus for adults. Curt Cloninger is an actor who performs monologues at Christian conferences and churches across the country. I've been fortunate to see him perform several times. In one sketch he portrays many common ideas of what God should be. Perhaps the most poignant is of God as a waiter, complete with tray and notepad. He seems to be talking to someone and writing down a list of "needs" from the unseen person's prayer. The customer asks for a new car. God wants to talk, but the customer seems to have left after making his request.

We ask God for the strangest things. New clothes, a fast car, good grades, and we pile our wants on top of wants. Sometimes we pray for healings of loved ones and then get angry with God when grandpa dies anyway.

"Speak, God, your servant is listening." It's a simple prayer. The hard part is to say it and then actually listen.

Us:	Here You go, God.
God:	What's this?
Us:	It's my list.
God:	List of what?
Us:	Stuff I need.
God:	You need all this?
Us:	This is what it takes to get ahead in the world today.
God:	What about My list?
Us:	What?
God:	I have a list too.
Us:	Am I being punished or something?

Praying the simple prayer is not easy. The dangerous part of asking God to speak to you or to "make my heart as Thine" is that He might actually do it!

You can't say, "Your servant is listening," and then not listen. Part of the practice of the presence is to actually open yourself up to what might be said. Listen with your heart. Listen with your ears. Listen with your very soul.

Step 5: All Around

This practice of the Presence of God is somewhat hard at the outset, yet pursued faithfully, it works imperceptibly within the soul most marvelous effects; it draws down God's grace abundantly, and leads the soul insensibly to the ever-present vision *of God, loving and beloved, which is the most spiritual and most real, the most free and most life-giving manner of prayer.* —Brother Lawrence

Once again, *this is not easy.* Brother Lawrence told us this twice. This process of acquiring the presence of God takes practice. It takes discipline. It takes falling and getting up again. In a world full of instant gratification, this requires patience.

One of the key words in the passage above is "imperceptibly." God will do great works in you, and you may be completely unaware of it. Remember when we talked about those people who just seem to be at peace with themselves all the time. If you were to ask those people who are in your circle, "How do you do it?" most would not have a clue. But look at their lives, and you'll see that God is blessing them imperceptibly.

God is all around us all the time. God is not something that we have to go and find, yet we spend hundreds of dollars and hours searching for Him. Brother Lawrence said that when we continually practice this presence, when we are changed "imperceptibly," God's grace will be "drawn down" and will lead our souls to the ever-present vision of God.

You cannot go and find. You can only connect to what's already there.

Step 6: Oneness with God

Remember that to attain to this state, we must mortify the senses, inasmuch as no soul, which takes delight in earthly things, can find full joy in the Presence of God; to be with Him we must leave behind the creature.
—Brother Lawrence

There are those who eat to survive and those who eat for pleasure. I'm pretty sure that heaven smells like chocolate-chip cookies. I hope heaven's welcome station is basically a Krispy Kreme doughnut shop where I get to sit at a table with Jesus and drink coffee, and we each get half a dozen.

I think these are more of a celebration of life than a means to acquire the presence. To really experience the presence we must "leave behind the creature." Perhaps it might help to think of "the creature" as creature comforts. We must leave behind our ideas of what is pleasing based on the physical. We must think not in terms of our own senses but of the soul. The soul does not need food or blankets or medicine. The soul needs oneness with God.

The presence is not something we feel physically. It is an interaction of the soul with God. We will not attain it by drugs or drinking. We will not attain it through music or art or anything that has to do with enlivening the senses or dulling them. Art and music and dance ... these things may open doorways, but they are not our means of acquiring God's presence.

or loaned to set in gods

When we die, we will be freed from our limitations. Right now we are human, and we are limited by human senses. We see, smell, hear, touch, and taste. When we die, we will not have these limitations. Perhaps after we die, there are 876 senses. Perhaps there is an infinite number of senses that we gain when we lose the five. God is not human. God is so far beyond our understanding that we can't put into words what He is. If we want to connect with that ... if we want to have a "union of the soul" with our Creator, then it's going to happen when we put away the things that keep us down and simply open ourselves to the presence. It's going to happen without any accouterments. It's going to happen when we are ready.

to talk about how loyal Job video?

09

The Benefits of the Presence

The first benefit which the soul receives from the Presence of God is that faith grows more alive *and active in all the events of life, particularly when we feel our need, since it obtains for us the succor of His grace when we are tempted, and in every time of trial. Accustomed by this practice to take faith as guide, the soul, by a simple remembrance, sees and feels God present, and calls upon Him freely and with assurance of response, receiving the supply of all its needs.*
—Brother Lawrence

Ever notice that God seems to be our last resort? We have problems at work, and every day seems to get worse. We talk with friends, maybe we talk with a professional counselor, but it always seems that we wait until we are kneeling down in the rain screaming at the sky to finally say, "God, why is this happening?" Or more likely ... "God, why are You doing this to me?"

We see the damage caused by the hurricane on CNN,

and we wonder, "Where is God when that happens?"

We listen to those atheists that we know who smugly say, "If there is a God, why does He permit so much suffering in the world?"

When we practice the presence, something happens. Our faith grows stronger. Brother Lawrence said it becomes "more alive." (That's assuming our faith was alive in the first place.) Whatever faith you have, the practice of the presence will make it grow.

If we practice the presence, our faith will get stronger. We might just learn to go to God before everything falls apart around us. If we practice the presence, we understand that God is with us when we fall. And God is with us when we stand up again.

Faith is all you have when it comes to God. You can never actually win an argument with someone who says, "Prove to me that God exists." There is no proof. It's all about faith. Tony Campolo, the liberal evangelist, (no, not an oxymoron) when questioned about how he could possibly believe in a God when there wasn't one single piece of evidence, simply said, "I decided to." Faith is our choice. God gives us that. God drenches us with His very presence all the time. We are surrounded by Him.

When our faith is stronger, we tend to look not at the damage caused by the hurricane but at the people who are helping the victims dig out. We might help with donations and prayers and even take the time to lend a hand (literally). But it is our faith that moves us to do so. When our faith is stronger, we will remember the last time we went through a rough patch, and we will be able to draw on the lessons learned from that.

A simple prayer from our souls to God will make us feel connected. We will feel the assurance that God is in charge, that God will take all things (good and bad) and make them work together. We will find comfort in knowing that those poor people on television are in the arms of their Creator.

Like many people, I sat transfixed in front of my television on September 11. I was actually on my way out the door to go to the airport when my wife called and said, "Don't go." "Why?" I asked. "Turn on the TV," she said. I don't recall moving from that spot for the rest of the day.

In the days that followed, I started to think on the idea that death is something that happens alone. It is, for the most part, a solitary act. Even if a person is surrounded by his loved ones in a hospital bed with tubes running in and out of his body, he still goes through the act of dying by himself. If you listen to the stories of people who claim to have died and come back, they will even talk about traveling into the great light alone. But the World Trade Center was not like that.

The release of thousands of souls all at once must have been like a party. Picture thousands of souls traveling up all at once ... together flying at full speed, unencumbered by bodies, pains, stress, and all the other things that weigh us down. They fly up, straight into the arms of God. To them ... it must have been a celebration.

One of the important parts to remember is that faith *grows*. You will not have some kind of super faith when you begin the presence. Children do not jump up from infancy and dance. Kids do not climb on a bike and ride the first time without skinning their knees. Faith *grows*. You failed tests and learned to study harder; you drank to excess and spent a day with your head in the toilet and didn't drink that way anymore. Faith *grows*. We must learn to use our faith. Faith *grows* and becomes more alive when we learn to connect with God. When God is a part of our everyday lives, our faith becomes central to who we are. We no longer doubt. We no longer expect black and white. We learn that some questions have no answers and others may not be answered right away.

Our hope grows in proportion as our knowledge; and in measure as our faith by this holy practice penetrates into the hidden mysteries of God, in like measure it finds in Him a beauty beyond compare, surpassing infinitely that of earth, as also that of the most holy souls and angels. Our hope grows and waxes ever stronger, sustained and enheartened by the fulness of the bliss, which it aspires to and even already tastes in part. —Brother Lawrence

Once you understand that you can't understand, then you begin to understand. We have to come to grips with the fact that we are not God (see chapter 5). God is a being so far beyond our knowing that we cannot possibly comprehend what He is. The good news is that it is not necessary for us to understand the Creator in order for us to love the Creator.

Again, we are limited by our senses. Everything we know or believe we know is based on those five senses. What does God look like? What does God smell like? God cannot be defined by our senses. Those questions are a first step (a requirement) before we can start to think of God in terms of something we can never fully understand until we are with Him.

When we practice the presence of God, we can sometimes tap into that idea. We can connect, at least a little; and that "connection" can change our lives—mentally, spiritually, and physically. We find in that moment a "beauty beyond compare" as Brother Lawrence put it. A presence that is beyond our understanding. God is a being of love. Pure love. God is the creator of joy. Pure joy.

Our hope increases as we come to realize that these moments of connection are like a pinprick of light through a dark shroud. Those wonderful moments of "virtual union" (see chapter 7) are one drop of water going over Niagara Falls. This is what is in store for us. When we come face to face with the Creator of the universe, that shroud is removed from our heads, and we stand at the bottom of Niagara Falls. How can our hopes not increase?

Hope breathes into the will a distrust of things seen, and sets it aflame with the consuming fire of Divine love; for God's love is in very truth a consuming fire, burning to ashes all that is contrary to His will: the soul thus kindled cannot live save in the Presence of God, and this Presence works within the heart a consecrated zeal, a holy ardor, a violent passion to see this God known and loved, and served and worshiped by all His creatures.
—Brother Lawrence

The practice of the presence teaches us that we can find joy beyond our senses. That inner joy comes from God. We can use music and art and the divine smell of baking cookies as doorways, but the true joy is going to come from simply opening the door to our hearts and letting the presence of God in. Once we do that, God is going to make it impossible for us to find joy the way we did before.

We are all searching. We are searching for purpose in our lives. We are searching for the meaning of our existence. We are searching for answers. Unfortunately, sometimes that search takes us down the wrong path and leads us to try things that are not healthy or necessary to our (and His) purposes. One of the benefits of the presence of God is that we find we are already filled. We find that sense of meaning without destroying ourselves. We find that sense of purpose without screwing up our relationships. We find ourselves wanting to feel that way all the time but wanting to share it with others. The presence of God is too much for one soul, and it must be passed around.

By the practice of the Presence of God, by steadfast gaze *on Him, the soul comes to a knowledge of God, full and deep, to* an Unclouded Vision: *all its life is passed in unceasing acts of love and worship, of contrition and of simple trust, of praise and prayer, and service; at times indeed life seems to be but one long unbroken practice of His Divine Presence.*
—Brother Lawrence

Not everybody gets this far. Brother Lawrence said that we may not ever achieve a "perfect union," but that should not stop us from the attempt. There is benefit to the attempt. When we practice the presence, we find that those "God moments," the pieces of life that make it seem like all is right with the world, will come upon us more frequently. We learn that the times we are down in the hole of despair are temporary, and we can feel God in both places.

Peter (the disciple who Jesus called The Rock) tells us:

> For this very reason, make every effort to add to your faith goodness; and to goodness, knowledge; and to knowledge, self-control; and to self-control, perseverance; and to perseverance, godliness; and to godliness, brotherly kindness; and to brotherly kindness,

love. For if you possess these qualities in increasing measure, they will keep you from being ineffective and unproductive in your knowledge of our Lord Jesus Christ.
(2 Pet. 1:5-8)

Years ago I remember driving home from my grandfather's house in a blizzard. I followed my uncle's car, both of us believing that if we could just make it to the highway, we would be fine. I remember the grip I had on the steering wheel. I remember that the snow was so thick that each pass of the wiper blade revealed his taillights for just a moment. Eventually we found the entrance to the highway only to discover that the road and the visibility were no better there. We pulled off the highway and into a cheap motel where my aunt and uncle, my wife and I, and our infant daughter stayed the night.

I remember waking up the next morning and stepping out into that parking lot. There was so much that I didn't see the night before. I didn't see the trucks behind the hotel parked in a line. I didn't see the coffee shop attached to the side of the hotel. I didn't see the "closed for renovation sign" on the door. (The manager had opened his place to us and several other travelers in spite of the renovations.) So much was different than it had been the night before.

We go through life this way. We're peering through the windshield hoping to catch just enough of a glimpse of the car ahead of us to know we are still on the road. We go through life unaware that our knuckles are white, and we clench up trying to steer ourselves in the direction we want to go. We become so focused on our own needs that we fail to see the kindness and generosity people are extending to us.

The practice of the presence of God aims us toward that "unclouded vision," that morning after the storm when we see the world in a new light and with a new attitude. We see things with a sense of gratitude and relief and anticipate getting back on the road now that it is safe to travel.

The benefits of connecting into the presence come not from what God gives us but from a strengthening of our knowledge of what is already there.

10

Gathered Thoughts

On Your Mark ...

You are young, my brethren; profit therefore I beseech you from my confession, that I cared too little to employ my early years for God. Consecrate all yours to His Love. If I

*had only known Him sooner, if I had only had some one
to tell me then what I am telling you, I should not have so
long delayed in loving Him. Believe me, count as lost each
day you have not used in loving God.* —Brother Lawrence

Start now.

Nicholas Herman did not become Brother Lawrence
until he was in his fifties. Most people would say that's
too old for a career change.

But there are no written records of anyone on their
deathbed saying, "I wish I had spent more time at the
office."

So you can start now—whatever age you are.

This is not to say that you should quit your job and
become a monk or a missionary if that is not where
God is calling you. More than likely you can do
amazing things for God in your chosen profession.
Begin leading a spiritual life. Begin the practice of
connecting to God all the time, and you will see how
it affects your decision-making and your long-range
plans for yourself.

Start now.

See where the practice leads you, and follow there.
Who you are is for you to decide. God has a plan,
sure, but you get to decide whether or not you
are going to go along. Many people start out their

adulthood with what they think is a full knowledge of who they are and where they are going. Then they discover that maybe those plans weren't theirs but someone else's. They discover new ideas and new thoughts and new actions that let them experience life in a way they were never allowed to before.

College for some is like waking up from a long sleep. You never knew what was out there. Some people don't experience this "awakening" until after they are out of college.

The popular song "Wear Sunscreen" by Baz Luhrmann includes the words: *Don't feel guilty if you don't know what you want to do with your life./The most interesting people I know didn't know at twenty-two what they wanted to do with their lives./Some of the most interesting forty-year-olds I know still don't.*

Brother Lawrence would add, "But don't even try it without God."

Leading a spiritual life and spending time practicing the presence of God (even if you never come close to the level of "presence" that Brother Lawrence achieved) will make life better. Will it make you more successful? Who knows? But with God at your side, the ride will definitely be more enjoyable.

Start now.

You're Fired

I am in the hands of God, and He has His own good purposes regarding me; therefore I trouble not myself for aught that man can do to me. If I cannot serve God here, elsewhere I shall find a place wherein to serve Him.
—Brother Lawrence

There is one story about the life of Brother Lawrence that says he was once called on the carpet and threatened to be kicked out of the monastery. This was later discovered to be a mistake, and Brother Lawrence himself was said to be innocent of whatever charges had been brought against him. Instead of putting up a defense or arguing his case, he simply said: "If I cannot serve God here, elsewhere shall I find a place wherein to serve Him."

This line later turned up in some of his writings. To be so faithful, to be so sure of the idea that God has a plan for our lives that we could take the threat of an unprovoked firing or an unfair eviction with such grace seems completely foreign to us. Brother Lawrence did just that.

I was fired from one job in my lifetime. The humiliation and pain stung. I spent months asking God, "Why?" I spent weeks on my knees demanding to know what was going on, what the plan was. I was angry, and I wanted answers. I got none.

There was no still small voice. There was no burning

bush. There was only the silence of my living room, my bedside, my car. I once even walked out into the ocean (a place where I like to pray) and stood there with water up to my neck, vowing that I was really listening this time and that if God would just give me a hint of what was going on, I'd shut up about it. I came in thirty minutes later, wrinkled and salty and feeling more alone.

Eventually I got the idea that I wasn't in charge. I started to pray one-line prayers. Rather than demanding answers from the Creator of the universe, I simply started repeating ...

God, I will go where You send me. Amen.

God, I am Your servant. Amen.

I'd like to say things started turning around immediately. But that wasn't how God worked.

A few months later I was gainfully employed at a small church in Florida. As I look back on it and as I talk with people at the church, I realize that there were so many pieces of the puzzle that led to my taking a position with this church. None of them were in place when I lost my job. Over time things started to fit together, some of them having nothing to do with me or the church where I was hired, but all of them eventually leading to the most supportive and rewarding place I have ever worked.

My friend Bob and I wrote a prayer last year about waking up on a cold, gray, post-winter morning when you have the flu and still thanking God.

> God, it is raining again.
> The sky is the color of the pavement.
> It's starting to get cold again.
> Eventually it's going to be February.
> February feels like a hangover.
> I woke up this morning, and I had coffee.
> I have air in my lungs and shoes on my feet
> and breakfast in my belly.
> I have people who love and respect me.
> I work with Your children.
> I work for the Creator of the universe.
> What can the weather do for me except give
> me a cold?
> I have Day-Quil, and I work for the Creator of
> the universe.
> That's enough.
> Amen.

The book of Psalms has some good prayers about "what aught that man can do to me."

Psalm 118—Neverending (author's paraphrase)

> Say thank you to God
> God's love does not end.
> Let the warring nations say,
> God's love does not end.
> Let the jocks, the bullies, and those in
> detention say,

God's love does not end.
Let the band geeks, the dorks, the dweebs,
and the nerds say,
God's love does not end.
Let all parents, teachers, principals, and hall
monitors say,
God's love does not end.
I was so angry and hurt I thought I would
explode,
But God was with me.
If God is with me, what can puny humans do?
Trust your God, not your television.
Trust your God, not millionaires.
I was surrounded on all sides
Like bees. Like fire. They surrounded me.
God was there. God listened.
These people don't bother me anymore.
I was hanging from the edge by my fingertips.
God reached down and helped me.
God is my strength.
God is my song.
There is a party going on, and God is the
reason for the celebration.
God has not only shown me the door to the
rest of my life,
He is holding it open for me.
God made this day.
This day. This moment. This here and now.
God made it.
Celebrate.
Say thank you to God.
God's love does not end.
Amen.

Trust God and practice His presence. If it turns out that you cannot serve Him where you are, He will put you in place where you can.

Evidence of Things Unseen

If you would go forward in the spiritual life, you must avoid relying on the subtle conclusions and fine reasonings of the unaided intellect. Unhappy they who seek to satisfy their desire therein! The Creator is the great teacher of Truth. We can reason laboriously for many years, but fuller far and deeper is the knowledge of the hidden things of faith and of Himself. —Brother Lawrence

This is what you know versus what you "know."

You can't argue with an atheist. Atheists demand— and will only be satisfied with—physical proof, and that's the one thing you can't give in a theology that requires you to take things on faith.

Do you know someone who "reasons laboriously"? Someone who sits at the staff meeting and has to think and rethink every idea until it's gone? These people play a necessary role in business. They are the ones who can find the flaws before the process begins, thus saving thousands of dollars down the line.

When it comes to faith ... laborious reasoning is of no use. We accept that God is because God *is*. We accept that God has a plan for our lives because He *does*. We believe that God is above us, beneath us, beside us, around us, and inside us ... because God *is* above us, beneath us, beside us, around us, and inside us. That's not an arguable point for us. We believe because we believe.

When we start to feel like we are lesser Christians because we cannot offer proof ... When we start to feel like we failed God because we have questions of our own ... We are reasoning laboriously. Faith is simple. We are constantly complicating it in new and various ways.

God says, "Believe," and we do. (Well, we should.) Any questions or doubts are of our own creation.

We are a society that must touch the wood when the sign says "wet paint." We want the same kind of proof with our supreme being. We're not going to get that. There are those who can flat-out see the work of the hand of God in their lives. Those who reason laboriously have more trouble doing so. Be patient with these people. Eventually they will come around.

Place Your Game Pieces on "Go"

Before beginning any task I would say to God, with childlike trust: "O God, since Thou art with me, and it is Thy will that I must now apply myself to these outward duties, I beseech Thee, assist me with Thy grace that I may continue in Thy Presence; and to this end, O Lord, be with me in this my work, accept the labor of my hands, and dwell within my heart with all Thy Fulness."
—Brother Lawrence

Start with God. Gen 3:22?

Which t how many?

This is not just a happy thought.

Pray before you get up in the morning. Pray before you go to work. Pray before you begin a task. Pray before you play a pick-up game in the park. Pray before you ask for a raise. Pray before you ask her out on a date. Pray before you cook. Pray before you clean. Pray before you go to sleep. Pray before you get up again.

If we are truly serious about asking for the continuous presence of God, then we have to start at the beginning. Brother Lawrence wrote that we must not only ask God's presence when we begin but ask that God remain with us while we are doing the task and ask that God be a part of that task.

Try this prayer.

> God,
> You are completely here.
> Make Your presence known as I begin.
> Stay with me as I work.
> Let what I do be acceptable to You.
> Amen.

Try repeating this small prayer, or come up with something equally simple to begin your tasks with. Pray silently. Pray out loud. Use the fancy church words if that helps you feel the connection better or just think on God as you begin. This is the beginning of the presence. If you miss this, it will be even harder to connect later.

What God Wants

Moreover, as I wrought, I would continue to hold familiar converse, offering to Him my little acts of service, entreating the unfailing succor of His grace. —Brother Lawrence

God does not expect too overmuch of us. God says, "Love me. Love each other." Most lessons after that are pretty negotiable depending on the denomination. "Love me. Love each other."

You get a bonus when you consider that Jesus said, "When you have done this to the least of My brothers, you have done it for Me as well."

Brother Lawrence wrote a lot about continuous prayer and being continuously connect to the Creator. He challenged us to think on God continuously. You've prayed at the beginning of the task; now you are being asked to connect to God while you are doing the task.

What is the task? Just living your life every day can take the life out of you sometimes. You can go with a group to another state and spend a week fixing and painting a playground for homeless children, help plant the garden that will grow vegetables, hold the four-year-old on your shoulders so he can stuff the ball in the Little Tikes basket. It's pretty easy to think about God in these circumstances if you're out there being the servant.

What about the "little acts of service"? What about those moments you can let God in on your average Thursday?

Ever tell someone at work they looked nice? Ever stop and comment on the pictures a coworker has on his desk? Do you know the name of the person who cleans up after you've gone home? Ever buy coffee for the person behind you in the drive-through and then drive away really fast so they can't thank you? What about letting someone pull out of a parking lot in front of you?

If our task is simply living each day and not feeding the world, there are ways that we can offer God these "little acts" all the time. The trick is that we do them for God, not to make ourselves feel better.

If God says, "Whom shall I send?" We say, "God, send me." There is an obligation that goes along with that. We actually have to go.

To say "I am the Lord's servant" implies that you may actually have to serve.

When we "go" or "serve," even when it might hurt or be an inconvenience or take our free time or even get us killed, that's when we know we are doing it for God. Anyone can do it when it's fun. Can you perform the "little acts of service" when they're simply inconvenient or mean getting out of bed on a Sunday morning when the covers feel so good?

And "the succor of His grace." How sweet that must be! I think the grace of God feels like a glass of iced tea after you've just finished mowing the lawn on a hot August afternoon. The grace of God feels like putting your stocking feet up on the heat register after coming in from shoveling the driveway. Someone warm smiles and hands you a cup of coffee, and you look out at the snow. (Not the gray, slushy snow but the big, white, fluffy flakes they write songs about.)

If we work to maintain that connection throughout the day, if we consciously focus our minds and live our lives in His presence, then we will feel the succor of His grace.

Trivial Pursuit: The God Edition

That we should feed and nourish our souls with high notions of God, which would yield us great joy in being devoted to Him. That we ought to quicken—i.e., to enliven—our faith. That it was lamentable we had so little; and that instead of taking faith *for the rule of their conduct, men amused themselves with trivial devotions, which changed daily.* —Conversations

I attended a conference some years ago where one of the workshops was titled "Making the Bible Come

Alive!" The convention organizers had named the workshop, and the speaker had taken a red magic marker and written beneath the title on the sign ... "(Not that we're assuming it's dead or anything like that)."

We must enliven our faith. Too often we approach our faith as if it is something we do only on Sundays. The rest of the week we must live in the "real world."

There is a big difference between the way the world works and the way God wants us to live.

The world teaches us that to get ahead you step on those who are in your way, look out for yourself, get yours first, do it yourself because no one else is going to do it for you, protect your back, play the game, work the politics, grab all you can because you never know when it's not going to be there.

God says to look out for each other, help each other up when you fall, get yours last, trust God, back each other up, don't be loose with the truth, don't take more than is yours.

What would happen if we took our faith into the world? What if when the rest of the lunch table started boss-bashing, we chose not to participate in that conversation? What would happen if instead of passing the blame for a client lost, we actually took responsibility? What if ... what if ... what if ...

You might think, "I have to do what I have to do in order to survive. That's the way things are done." But aren't all the excuses just "trivial devotions"?

Do you think if you live as God wants you to that He's not going to take care of you? Do you think that if you help someone up from a fall that God's not going to do the same for you?

God is not the last resort. We break. We fall. We slip. We mess up. We watch our lives come apart, and then when it's all over, we finally say, "Hey, God? Could I get a little help please?"

Live by faith. Enliven your faith. Don't lie. Don't cheat. Don't steal. Don't gossip. Don't manipulate.

Is someone else who does all these things going to get the promotion ahead of you? Probably. Could you live with yourself if you got the promotion by lying, cheating, stealing, manipulating?

There's a reason the people in the corner offices spend so much time and money on therapy. The number of stress-related heart attacks in corporate America is staggering.

Play honest. Play fair. Play hard. You will succeed. You may have to adjust your personal definition of success, but you will succeed. God takes care of His own.

I'm glad in God, far happier than you would ever guess—happy that you're again showing such strong concern for me. Not that you ever quit praying and thinking about me. You just had no chance to show it. Actually, I don't have a sense of needing anything personally. I've learned by now to be quite content whatever my circumstances. I'm just as happy with little as with much, with much as with little. I've found the recipe for being happy whether full or hungry, hands full or hands empty. Whatever I have, wherever I am, I can make it through anything in the One who makes me who I am. (Phil. 4:10-13, MSG)

A Closet Full of Skeletons

That this trouble of mind had lasted four years, during which time he had suffered much; but that at last he had seen that this trouble arose from want of faith, and that since he had passed his life in perfect liberty and continual joy. That he had placed his sins betwixt him and God, as it were, to tell Him that he did not deserve His favors, but that God still continued to bestow them in abundance. —Conversations

Brother Lawrence had a past. Much is debated about what his "sins" were, but they were enough to keep him convinced that he was bound for hell when he died and that all his current problems and predicaments were the result of those sins.

God knows everything. God knows who you are down deep in your soul. There is nothing that is hidden from Him. Brother Lawrence must have, at some point, just put it all out there and confessed it to God. He reached down into the places that we don't talk about and said, "Here it is. I don't deserve to be loved, blessed, or appreciated." God saw this pile, then took His bag of blessings and "continued to bestow them in abundance."

Whatever it is that is creeping into the back of your mind, God already knows. But you have to be able to put it "betwixt" you and your Creator. You can't hide it. You can't deny it exists, especially from the One who made all things in the first place.

Confession is good for the soul. God will look at the pile of baggage that you put before Him, and He will sweep it away. Dump it. Run it through a garbage disposal. Then God will look at the empty parts of your soul. Those spaces that have been taken up too long by guilt and fear and pain, and He will fill them with His love and peace and joy. But until you are ready to empty those spots, you can't have the good stuff.

Don't let fear make you hold onto what you don't need anymore. I have always been amazed at the number of battered women who return again and again to the abuser. The fear of leaving so far outweighs the fear of staying that they wind up being abused over and over.

God is not going to beat you up. God is not standing at the gates of heaven with a bucket full of lightning bolts with your name on them. He does not work that way. God is standing there with a broom and a dustpan, saying, "We can clean this up." He is standing there with His arms open and a warm washrag in His hand waiting to wash the dirt from your face and make you clean.

God is waiting with a mountain of blessings reserved just for you, but you have to make room for them.

You Silly Little Pickle

That he had so often experienced the ready succors of divine grace upon all occasions, that from the same experience, when he had business to do, he did not think of it beforehand; but when it was time to do it, he found in God, as in a clear mirror, all that was fit for him to do. That of late he had acted thus, without anticipating care; but before the experience above mentioned, he had used it in his affairs. —Conversations

When I taught Sunday school, my students were very fond of VeggieTales. (If you are unfamiliar with this video series, imagine *Toy Story*-type animation involving talking vegetables acting out Bible lessons written by folks with a strong love of Monty Python. No, I'm not kidding.)

At the end of one show, on hearing that "with God all things are possible," Larry the Cucumber asks,

"What if I want to be a chicken? Can God make me a chicken?"

Of course, Larry learns that is not what the verse means, but instead that whatever God wants us to do, we can do.

If God wants something to happen, it can happen. If we say, "Nope, it'll never work," then we are going against what God wants. God will make it happen. God will give you the tools.

When I say "Moses," most of you will think of either Charlton Heston in *The Ten Commandments* or *The Prince of Egypt*. Moses. Strong and handsome. Standing heroically on the mountain. Letting the winds whip his long hair like a holy blow dryer.

Read the story. Moses tried to get out of the job several times.

God:	Go.
Moses:	Who am I to do such a thing?
God:	I'll go with you; now go.
Moses:	But who do I say sent me?
God:	Tell them I did.
Moses:	What if they don't believe me?
God:	(does some cool special effects with a snake)
Moses:	I'm not a good public speaker.
God:	I'll tell you what to say when you get there.

Moses:	Can't You get someone else?
God:	Fine, take your brother with you. Now go.

God has been with you up until now. Why would He leave you to yourself? Once you start practicing the presence of God, you will be able to feel it when you most need it. You will be able to draw on that experience and apply it to whatever is before you. You will gain strength. You will gain courage. You will feel that I-am-not-alone feeling when you face your toughest hurdles.

Whatever God wants you to do, you can do.

God said so.

No Admittance

That many do not advance in the Christian progress because they stick in penances and particular exercises, while they neglect the love of God, which is the end*. That this appeared plainly by their works, and was the reason why we see so little solid virtue.* —Conversations

This is an old story that I heard many years ago. I have no idea where it came from, but in an effort to give credit where credit is due, it is not mine.

> Once upon a time there was a man who went to a church for the very first time. The people there were polite and nice. When

they stood up to sing, the man sang with joy and love at the top of his lungs. Many of the people turned and looked at him, but they said nothing. During the time of greeting, the man shook hands heartily and laughed out loud. He even hugged a few strangers. During the sermon, the man shouted "amen" several times. When the service was over, a few elders of the church took him quietly and discreetly aside and told him that this was not how they were accustomed to behaving and that he might want to find a church that was more suited to his personality. After everyone had gone home, the man was sitting, dejected, on the steps of the church and wondering what he had done wrong.

It was then that Jesus came by and sat down on the step next to him, put a reassuring hand on his shoulder, and said, "Don't worry about it. I've been trying to get in for years."

Have you ever been to a church where the people were so worried about being religious that they forgot to be God's children?

We get bogged down in our rules and regulations, and then we wonder why there is a decline in membership. Those wanting to become new members of a church will sometimes be asked to attend a year's worth of classes before they can join! Members are told they can just "attend" church, or they can reach for some higher form of membership that requires more time, more money, more prayer, more meetings.

Years ago I taught a confirmation class at a church in Florida. I was given a curriculum and told how to teach the class. I was also given a test that each person in the class had to take and pass before they could join the church. (No mention was made as to what I was supposed to do if one of the students didn't happen to score above a 50 percent.) The first Sunday I took the confirmation test to the adult Sunday school class and gave it to a roomful of parents, adults, and long-time members. Half the class could not pass the test they expected their children to pass in order to become a member.

When the "guide to giving" shows up in the membership packet, when the manual on parking procedures is thicker than the Bible, when the fellowship committee starts making rules about who can and can't have the "good cookies," maybe we are starting to get stuck in our "penances and particular exercises."

God is here. Connect.

There are not a lot of ways to make that simpler.

Shortcuts and Other Painful Detours

He told me that all consists in one hearty renunciation of everything which we are sensible does not lead to God. That we might accustom ourselves to a continual conversation with Him, with freedom and in simplicity. That we need only to recognize God intimately present with us, to address ourselves to Him every moment, that we may beg His assistance for knowing His will in things doubtful, and for rightly performing those which we plainly see He requires of us. —Conversations

Let's talk about behavior. There are things we do that do not lead us to God.

Let's put that another way ... there are things we do that we are perfectly aware do not lead us to God.

You cannot be perfect. That's not even the issue. The issue is that there are things that we do that will get in the way of the presence.

Will these behaviors get in the way of us spending eternity with Him? I believe in the grace of God. There is no such thing as "cheap grace" to me. There is only grace. We get the grace. We get to go in. All of us.

That, without being discouraged on account of our sins, we should pray for His grace with a perfect confidence, as relying upon the infinite merits of our Lord Jesus Christ. That God never failed offering us His grace at each action. —Conversations

Sometimes we know we are doing something stupid, and we do it anyway. We willfully go off and behave in a way that we are "sensible does not lead to God." We are perfectly aware that what we are about to do is not in our best interest. But Brother Lawrence draws the distinction between behavior we know is unhealthy and behavior we don't know is unhealthy. Can a man raised in a house that never believed, never taught about Jesus, never attended church be held accountable for not knowing? I don't think so.

But there are things that we do that will keep us from knowing the presence of God. We must strive to connect. We have to work at it. If that means giving up some of our ego or some of our anger or some of our prejudices or some of our unsafe behaviors in order to connect, then that is what we must do.

Go to Jail, Go Directly to Jail, Do Not Pass Go, Do Not Collect $200

When I had finished, I would examine how I had performed my duty: if I found well, I gave Him thanks; if ill, I besought His pardon, and without losing heart I set my spirit right, and returned anew unto His Presence, as though I had never wandered from Him.
—Brother Lawrence

Sometimes we fail.

The crash of great-grandma's gravy boat was like the starter pistol in a race of disaster. Dorothy was about to run to the table with a dishtowel when the potatoes began to boil over. Uncle Pete called from the dining room that the "little popper" on the turkey must have lied because it was nowhere near done in the center.

She pulled the potatoes off the burner and set them on a hot pad on the counter. Her cousin Kate asked, "Where are the mini-marshmallows for the sweet potato casserole?" Dorothy looked at the refrigerator and saw the list she was supposed to take with her to the store yesterday but forgot. Her youngest mentioned that the date on the bottom of the cranberry can was for Thanksgiving last year. Ben, her eldest, had brought his girlfriend to meet the family. The young lady mentioned in passing that her own mother made dinner rolls from scratch not the store-bought kind. She mentioned this just seconds before the smoke alarm went off because someone had closed the oven door on broil, and the store-bought brown-and-serve rolls were now more like black-and-throwaway rolls. Dorothy's sister, who brought exactly one pie for fifteen people and then plunked her butt in front of the parades, giggled but didn't get up.

Until about fifteen minutes ago, everything was perfect, and then it went south all at once. Dorothy reached into the oven to pull out the smoking rolls and grabbed the pan with her bare hand. She used some of her mother's "kitchen language" and dropped the pan on the floor. As she was running cold water over her burned fingers listening to no fewer than seven people call her name all at once, she began to cry.

Now let's look at life ...

Sometimes we make bad choices. We don't study for the final. We hang out with the wrong crowd. We fall in love with the wrong person. Sometimes we think they are the right person, and then it seems to go suddenly wrong. The professor who teaches the subject we most want to major in says we should probably find other ways to spend our time. We spend Sunday mornings vomiting up whatever we had on Saturday night because it didn't go well with the last four or five (or ten) drinks we had.

Sometimes no one brings food for the food drive. Sometimes we promise we will pray, show up for Bible study, go to church, give money, remember mom's birthday, and send a card to Aunt Gladys who's in the hospital because she broke her other hip.

Sometimes we just fail. With all the good intentions and all the prayers before, during, and after ... sometimes we just blow it.

God is not laughing at you. He will take you into His arms and let you cry against His shoulder. God may clean you up and send you back out there again, but He's not laughing at you. God is not angry. He's not keeping a list of the ways we screw up.

Dorothy's husband, Lloyd, took her into his arms after checking her burned fingers. Her youngest found some cortisone cream in the medicine cabinet. Uncle Pete cleaned the gravy off the tablecloth and set the boat back on the tray.

"Was loud but didn't break," he called out. Her son's girlfriend managed to scrape most of the black off the dinner rolls. The turkey had been carved of its cooked parts and was now back in the oven under the baking tent she had bought. Her sister joined the hug, and soon the rest of the family was encircling Dorothy and her burned fingers.

God is not laughing at you. God does not expect you to be perfect. God will help you pick up the pieces and start again.

God Thoughts

That in the beginning of his novitiate he spent the hours appointed for private prayer in thinking of God, so as to convince his mind of, and to impress deeply upon his heart, the divine existence, rather by devout sentiments, and submission to the lights of faith, than by studied reasonings and elaborate meditations. That by this short and sure method he exercised himself in the knowledge and love of God, resolving to use his utmost endeavor to live in a continual sense of His presence, and, if possible, never to forget Him more. —Conversations

Think about God. Seriously. Stick your finger in the book as a page marker and think about God. Give yourself a few minutes. Think about all that you know about God. Think about what you thought God was when you were a child. Go ahead. I'll give you a minute or two.

Brother Lawrence was not a well-educated man when he joined the monastery. For most monasteries, some proficiency in Latin is required before you are even considered. Brother Lawrence's education did not go far beyond the elementary level. Yet he spent years in classes with the young novitiates studying. (Remember he was probably in his fifties about this time.)

He learned how to pray. He learned what was expected of him in the time of prayer. He was given a set of rules and told not to deviate from them because that would not be prayer. "Do not pass go. Do not collect $200." *This* is what prayer is.

Brother Lawrence spent hours just thinking about God. In his own way he was defying the authority of the order that told him when to pray and how to pray. Brother Lawrence considered all thoughts about God to be prayer ... and all time was "prayer time."

Portions of "The Conversations" were not just from Brother Lawrence himself but also with his fellow monks who related things that Brother Lawrence had said. His simple means of sculpting his own soul was being noticed by those around him. His kind and peaceful manner was being emulated.

We are taught from a young age that kneeling and folding hands, or clasping hands around the dinner table, is the "position for prayer." As children we are taught the "prayer posture," but as adults we are free to explore the act of prayer. Kneeling with arms open and relaxed (a submissive posture) is a great way to pray. It allows you to relax without having to focus on your knees, back, or hands. It also allows you to be physically "open" and thus helps you to "open" spiritually.

The ABC network had a series some years back called *Nothing Sacred*. It was a wonderfully well-written show that was labeled as controversial because of its frank depiction of a priest in doubt. The young priest would pray sitting on an ergonomic kneeler that was a hit with corporations for about ten minutes. He set his kneeler in front of a large picture window that looked out over the city of Chicago. What a great place to pray. It made you think about King David pacing the roof of his palace at night.

We must learn how to pray, and then we must find our own pathway to prayer. In the ocean, on a rooftop, in a quiet closet, in the dark, on a hilltop at dawn. We must find our place to pray and then PRAY. Over and over. Again and again. Pray continually.

Eventually that place of sanctuary will become internalized, and we will find we can pray and connect to God anywhere whether we are in our "prayer place" or not.

God Latte

That when he had thus in prayer filled his mind with great sentiments of that infinite Being, he went to his work appointed in the kitchen (for he was cook to the society). There having first considered severally the things his office required, and when and how each thing was to be done, he spent all the intervals of his time, as well before as after his work, in prayer. —Conversations

God is caffeine. (Said like a true Starbucks fan.) How do you fill yourself? How do you get rid of the empty feeling that everyone experiences at one time or another and fill yourself up again?

What turns you on, gets your blood moving, energizes you? Music? Art? Dancing? Football?

God charges you. He may use a baseball game, the Rolling Stones, the Chicago Museum of Art, STOMP, or the New York Philharmonic, but if it is God who made all things and God who exists in all things, then that spirit, that energizing, comes from God.

Brother Lawrence found a way to "fill himself" through prayer.

Brother Lawrence planned his work. He went in each day and decided what he had to do, what tools he would need, and what times he would have to get his work done. Then he was able to better concentrate on God while he worked. I wonder if he liked working in the sandal shop better. The kitchen can be a chaotic place. The making and repairing of his fellow monks' footwear seems a much more conducive place to connect.

Your life is no doubt more chaotic than that of a seventeenth-century monk (even though most of the distractions and chaos are of our own creation). Being filled with the presence of God can make the day easier. Maybe "easier" is the wrong word. Being filled with God can give you the strength, patience, self-control, compassion, and determination to get you through the day that you are already having.

Begin early. Pray in your car rather than listening to talk-radio. Put on the "connection" music and focus your mind as you sit in rush-hour traffic. Think about God instead of the jelly donut you are going to miss if you don't get there early enough.

Keep that awareness of God going throughout the day. As you finish each phone call, take a deep breath before making the next one and focus on God and His presence and His blessings. Focus on God before. Focus on God during. Focus on God after.

God is here. Now. Already. Waiting.

Connect.

He's Making a List and Checking It Twice

That our sanctification did not depend upon changing our works, but in doing that for God's sake which we commonly do for our own. That it was lamentable to see how many people mistook the means for the end, addicting themselves to certain works, which they performed very imperfectly, by reason of their human or selfish regards. —Conversations

People have this bizarre tendency to see Christians in stereotypical ways. We are all either Mother Teresas or pulpit-pounding, screaming preachers.

We cannot be Mother Teresa. Only Mother Teresa could be Mother Teresa. She was such a servant. I sort of imagine her in heaven with her feet up while scantily clad hunky angels rub her feet and feed her grapes.

Once we get past people's ideas of the hypocritical pulpit-pounder, we find that mostly what keeps them from a relationship with God is fear. They don't think they are good enough. They don't believe that God can love and forgive them.

We think that if we cannot do what Mother Teresa did, then we may as well not try. We think because we went out and partied till we dropped on Friday that we have no business going to church on Sunday morning.

We believe that if we do something good, it's going to be written down in a big leather-bound book at the gates of heaven. Saint Peter is going to be standing there when we arrive and ask our names. He will look us up and run his finger down the list, checking our pluses and minuses, and if it all averages out, we get to go in.

God does not keep a scorecard. We do good works on earth because that's how we say "thank you" for the gifts God gave us. When we do any work on earth, we need to do it in the name of God—whether mundane tasks like taking out the garbage or community-changing events like organizing a food drive for homeless orphans. God is not going to look at one as better than the other. God is going to look and say, "Did you do it for you, or did you do it for Me?"

We screw up. Of course we screw up. We're human. We're not perfect. Nobody is perfect. OK, one guy was perfect, but they nailed Him to a piece of wood a long time ago, and we've been pretty consistent since then. Yeah, you tried. Did you do it for God and still make a mess of things? Yeah, that happens. God is beside you, above you, beneath you, and inside you, waiting for you to say, "I'm ready. Let's do this together and see what happens."

Falling on Deaf Ears

That we should establish ourselves in a sense of God's presence by continually conversing with Him. That it was a shameful thing to quit His conversation to think of trifles and fooleries. —Conversations

I happen to be a big fan of trifles and fooleries myself. Some of the best "God moments" I've ever had involved trifles and fooleries. I also have a belief that God likes trifles and fooleries ... just not when we let them get in the way.

We spend a lot of time worrying about the little

things, things that don't matter. We feel we must wear our Sunday best to church, when Jesus had one or two outfits tops. We spend a lot of time worrying about who should and should not be able to attend church. We get upset if someone is in our pew. We endlessly debate the topic of wine versus grape juice, and if we decide both, then who gets to be on the "tasting committee" to choose a wine. Wafers or wonder bread? King James Version or The Message? Pictures on the cover of the bulletin? Crayons available in the back for the little ones? Little ones ... keep them or send them out after the first hymn? Hymnals or projection screens? Traditional or praise music? And if you are going with her decision, then I'm just not going to show up at all!

I think somewhere God is in heaven looking down on these endless debates about how to worship Him, and He's saying:

"Helloooooooooo? Remember Me? Anybody want to talk?"

The new cushions in the parlor should be red and not blue. The senior pastor already wore that suit twice this month. Somebody took the good cookies that we were saving for the Pentecost reception. Her kid got to play Mary last year. Five typos in the bulletin this week ... can you believe that?

"Anybody? Anybody at all? Over heeeeeeere? It's Me!"
I hate this hymn. Who does she think SHE'S trying to

fool? Watch that kid ... he's going to try to take money out of the plate. Do you know what those darn kids have done now? He has a new girlfriend already? Poor Mrs. Harper, if she only knew.

"Still here. Read any good books lately? Come on, I made the universe over here. Is anybody listening? Anybody at all?"

He's Got the Whole World in His Hands

That as for the miseries and sins he heard of daily in the world, he was so far from wondering at them that, on the contrary, he was surprised that there were not more, considering the malice sinners were capable of; that, for his part, he prayed for them; but knowing that God could remedy the mischiefs they did when He pleased.
—Conversations

The world is a lot bigger now, and I wonder how far from wondering at the miseries and sins of the world could Brother Lawrence be if he had CNN. To be "surprised there are not more" is correct. It is a wonder that we don't blow ourselves up or annihilate each other daily.

We get worked up over whatever current emergency the media is telling us about. We no longer watch the news or read the papers to find out what's going on in the world. We look for ammunition, so that when "he" starts spouting off at the office, we'll be able to put him out of our misery.

We are instructed on who to hate, who to be suspicious of, who to trust, and who to blow off the face of the earth. So many of the things that were meant to unite us as a people are now serving to divide us as a nation.

It is possible to belong to a political party without hating the others. It is possible to be environmentally friendly without being a wacko. It is possible to be wrong once in a while.

When the O.J. Simpson trial began, networks devoted months of coverage, playing and replaying. Analyzing and reanalyzing. Hiring lip readers to find out what O.J. was whispering.

After September 11, news stations began devoting a significant portion of the screen to "the crawl"— small news banners providing the most up-to-date information available on whatever subject the anchorperson was not talking about at that moment.

God is in charge, but He has watched His children kill each other since He created them. Once He even started over, but we still are making the same mistakes. God is in charge, and if He wanted to, He could start over again tomorrow morning. So far, that hasn't happened. Our job is to connect with God at the start of each day to best find out what He wants us to do ... and then do that.

Let tomorrow worry about tomorrow ... today is hard enough.

Leveling Off at the Bottom

That he expected, after the pleasant days God had given him, he should have his turn of pain and suffering; but that he was not uneasy about it, knowing very well that as he could do nothing of himself, God would not fail to give him the strength to bear it. —Conversations

Nobody stays down forever.

Read the book of Psalms sometime and just look at how David (the "giant" killer, the king, the dancer, the songwriter, the adulterer) went from one extreme to the other. He spent pages wailing about how far down he was, and then wrote pages of soul-dancing lyrics.

You will fall down. You may be on your game right now and feel like things are going exactly your way, but you will fall. Likewise, if you feel like you've been living at the bottom of the well with the snakes, you will be lifted up.

This is how God meant it to be. Understand that. You don't stay down forever.

You will have car trouble the same time you have major appliances break down, which will coincide with the rumor at work that they are going to be letting people go.

You will have a call from out of the blue that says your resume is very good and would you be available for an interview the same week that guy you've been watching asks you out and you just found $20 in your old coat pocket.

These light and dark periods can last for weeks or months. What Brother Lawrence encouraged us to do was recognize that neither is permanent, that once you are in a "dark time," you cannot get yourself out of it, and God is not going to answer your prayer to do so. However, God will send you strength and patience and love to get through it.

Psalm 30—See Me, Hear Me, Heal Me
(author's paraphrase)

> I am going to shout your name from the
> highest place I can climb.
> You inspired my soul.
> You saw me down and picked me up.
> You didn't let THEM win.
> I was sure you would. I thought you were
> angry with me.
> You only stay angry for a moment.
> Your love will last me all through my life.
> I may cry at night. Bury my face in my pillow
> and sob.
> But joy comes in the morning.
> Joy comes in the morning.
> Joy comes in the morning.
> I was a heap on the floor, and now I'm
> dancing.

You have taken off my sick clothes and
dressed me in joy.
I will sing your name with my soul.
Silence? Never?
Amen.

The way to feel that strength and patience and love is
to connect with God during the good times and then
you will also be able to connect during the bad times.
Start now. Practice the presence. Then when you feel
like you are looking up at the sky from the bottom of
a well, you will know for certain that you are not alone
and that the dark is temporary.

Hey, Kids, What Time Is It?

*That it was a great delusion to think that the times of
prayer ought to differ from other times; that we are as
strictly obliged to adhere to God by action in the time of
action as by prayer in the season of prayer.*
—Conversations

Sunday is for God. The rest of the week is for me.
Right? And when I say Sunday, I mean Sunday
morning ... while I'm in church ... OK, while I'm in the
sanctuary. That's God's. That ninety-minute span is all
for You, big guy. Sunday afternoon is for football and
yard work and movies and, well, restful things. Sunday
is my day of rest, right?

People sometimes seem offended when you ask them
if they pray at times other than Sunday morning

worship. Do they even think about God other than on
Sunday mornings? Sure, when they need something
or traffic is bad.

The Bible says to remember the Sabbath and keep it
holy. That's all fine and good, but Brother Lawrence
said that is not the only time to pray. Sunday morning
is not your only "God time."

Some of Brother Lawrence's writings suggest that he
often got called on the carpet by fellow monks because
he did not seem to revere his prayer time above all
other activities. He did not "set aside" that time of
worship as being above all other times. The reason
he didn't was because, to him, the scheduled "prayer
time" was the same as any other.

God is present to us all the time. Shouldn't we be
willing to be there too?

On/Off

*That his prayer was nothing else but a sense of the presence
of God, his soul being at that time insensible to everything
but divine love; and that when the appointed times of
prayer were past, he found no difference, because he still
continued with God, praising and blessing Him with all
his might, so that he passed his life in continual joy; yet
hoped that God would give him somewhat to suffer when
he should grow stronger.* —Conversations

We do not go to the movies with the same attitude

that we go to a museum. Both involve looking at a picture. One moves. One, usually, does not. But our attitude changes. We watch movies for entertainment; we look at the paintings in a museum as art. It's a different mindset, isn't it?

If we can flip that mental switch when we go from a theater to a museum, why can't we flip the same switch when it involves prayer? Why does prayer have to be kneeling or sitting with your head bowed? Brother Lawrence believed that there was no difference between the time of prayer and the time of action. So flipping the switch is our responsibility, not God's.

In all my life I don't think I have ever prayed for God to give me something to suffer through. I think I have once or twice thanked God for a really, really bad day because I knew I would grow from it and because it strengthened my resolve. But I have never prayed for more suffering, nor do I know anyone who has.

Brother Lawrence apparently lived in such a state of perpetual joy that he said in conversation he hoped God would give him "somewhat to suffer" so that he could grow stronger.

Here's the amazing part about that. This is a truly amazing statement of faith. There was no question in the mind of this monk that God existed and that God was with him all the time. No questions. No doubts. So much so that he actually hoped God would give him something to suffer through so that he could grow stronger. He not only believed that he would grow stronger from suffering, but he wanted to grow stronger—and the only way for him to do that was through suffering, so he wanted God to give him some.

There are careers that will put you where you want to be and hand you a perfectly acceptable paycheck, and there are careers that will stretch your boundaries and make you grow and sweat for every dollar.

Brother Lawrence called us to grow. The Bible tells us not to be discouraged during hard times. But what sort of faith does it take to ask for them?

The Greatest of These

That the whole substance of religion was faith, hope, and charity, by the practice of which we become united to the will of God; that all besides is indifferent, and to be used as a means that we may arrive at our end, and be swallowed up therein, by faith and charity. —Conversations

The "substance" of religion—the material, the very stuff that religion is made up of—is faith, hope, and charity. Notice the good brother said nothing about showing up for new member classes. Nothing about finding the right denomination.

Religion is made up of faith, hope, and charity. Brother Lawrence was not specific about which religion. He didn't say Catholic, although he was one.

He didn't say Christian, Jew, or Muslim. Religion itself—our institutionalized system of beliefs and practices—is entirely made of faith, hope, and charity.

Where would we be if we actually made these three things our religion and treated them as a "means" to get to the presence of God?

Faith: To believe in something when everything else seems to point to the contrary. To believe in something without proof or evidence. To simply believe because that is what we choose to do.

Hope: To believe that it will be better. To shine a light in the darkest despair (ours or someone else's) and give light. Just a bit. Just enough.

Charity: To be generous. This is not necessarily about money. We can throw our change into the Salvation Army pot at Christmastime and still not be charitable. To be charitable is to give your time, your good works, your prayers, your help, and your hard-earned cash. Give of yourself but not for yourself. Give because it brings you closer to the presence of God.

Pathways to Prayer

Having found in many books different methods of going to God, and divers practices of the spiritual life, I thought this would serve rather to puzzle me than facilitate what I sought after, which was nothing but how to become wholly God's. This made me resolve to give the all for the all; so after having given myself wholly to God, that He might take away my sin, I renounced, for the love of Him, everything that was not He, and I began to live as if there was none but He and I in the world. —Brother Lawrence

God is the goal. Not in the sense that this is a race and that He is at the end of the track. God is the goal in the sense that becoming one with His presence is what we are after. When asked if he would write down his thoughts on how he came to the process of "practicing," Brother Lawrence wrote about reading many books. One only needs to browse though Borders' religion section to know that there are a great many books out there.

But if we believe that the end result is to connect to the presence of God, we are called to dispense of all those things that do not lead us to a connection. I cannot tell you or judge what brings you closer to God.

I have a friend who runs. I don't understand running. I don't run unless something is chasing me, and only then because I'm sure I'm not going to reason with it. My friend says that after a while running becomes like flying, and that feeling is a "God thing" to her.

I have another friend who listens to choral music. She puts on her headphones and a CD of a boys' choir singing in their perfect voices, and she blisses out. I have friends who love rock concerts and others who love silence.

Whatever brings you to God is a good thing. Once you are there, you may be asked to stay awhile. Connection happens, but it is seldom permanent. Books or music or art or sports—let these things be your means of connection. Once you are there, stay as long as you can. Practice this and you will be able to do it more often.

To live as though there is nothing but you and God in the world is difficult. Brother Lawrence was a monk; he could shut out the noise. He didn't have distractions to keep him from his "practice." Maybe it is time for us to look at our lives and identify what is "a distraction" and what is "of God."

I Wander as I Wonder

I worshiped Him the oftenest that I could, keeping my mind in His holy presence, and recalling it as often as I found it wandered from Him. I found no small pain in this exercise, and yet I continued it, notwithstanding all the difficulties that occurred, without troubling or disquieting myself when my mind had wandered involuntarily. I made this my business as much all the day long as at the appointed times of prayer; for at all times, every hour, every minute, even in the height of my business, I drove away from my mind everything that was capable of interrupting my thought of God. Such has been my common practice ever since I entered in religion; and though I have done it very imperfectly, yet I have found great advantages by it. These, I well know, are to be imputed to the mere mercy and goodness of God, because we can do nothing without Him, and I still less than any. —Brother Lawrence

My friend Bob in Ohio taught me the following prayer.

God, maker of heaven and earth, help me to stay focused on the thi- ... oh look, a chicken.

It's hard to stay focused, harder for some than others. We have little trouble paying attention to a movie on a screen, but put us in a quiet church while the minister leads us in prayer, and a great many people (myself included) will find their minds wandering to what's for lunch?, do I need to get the oil changed?, and how old is that lady now, one hundred?

Even Brother Lawrence had a tendency to let his mind wander. The only way to stop this is to practice. Take time during your day. Remind yourself to focus on God when you are standing in line at Starbucks. Focus on God when you are pumping your gas. Focus on God as you walk from your car into the office building. Start there. Start in those wandering times when your brain has nothing else do to. Many men will tell you they get great ideas when they are shaving. It's a time-consuming process that most men have done since their early teens. We do it all the time, and our minds can wander far, far away. What if we purposely focused on God during this time?

Focus on God while shaving? Why not? If the time

of business is no different than the time of prayer, then any time is OK to focus on God. Focus just for that moment when you are at a red light, cooking something in the microwave for lunch, or waiting for your Internet to boot up. Take these moments ... these brief moments in time ... and purposefully force yourself to think about God. Say a small prayer if you want, just a few words.

God, I am Your servant. Amen.

Green light. Go.

Try finishing the Bob prayer.

God, maker of heaven and earth, help me to stay focused on the things that are important to You. Amen.

Taking advantage of these little moments will make you more aware when larger ones are available. Spend a week praying while standing in line, and then during your time of prayer you will find your mind wanders less, the distractions are less annoying.

Chickens or not, this takes practice, and you will never accomplish it if you do not begin with the small moments.

In fine, by often repeating these acts, they become habitual, and the presence of God rendered as it were natural to us.
—Brother Lawrence

Braveheart

*In a conversation some days since with a person of piety, he
told me the spiritual life was a life of grace, which begins
with servile fear, which is increased by hope of eternal life,
and which is consummated by pure love; that each of these
states had its different stages, by which one arrives at last
at that blessed consummation. I have not followed all these
methods. On the contrary, from I know not what instincts, I
found they discouraged me. This was the reason why, at my
entrance into religion, I took a resolution to give myself up
to God, as the best return I could make for His love, and,
for the love of Him, to renounce all besides.*
—Brother Lawrence

God is love. Love is God. Everyone who loves knows
God. So the Scriptures tell us. Why would a God
made of pure love want a relationship based on fear?
Why do so many religions continually make longer
and longer lists of what you have to do to be accepted
by God (which usually means to be accepted by
them)? God is about love and joy and peace and more
joy and more love.

Rather than praying a lengthy prayer that says, "I
am nothing. I am worse than nothing, and I don't
deserve God, but if God will have me, I promise I
will do everything as outlined in section 3 paragraph
4 to make things right with Him," Brother Lawrence
simply said, "God, I am Yours."

When the angel Gabriel appeared to a frightened

teenage girl and said, "It's you. You're it. You are the one." Mary replied, "I am the Lord's servant."

There are so many religions in this world, so many that tell you they know exactly what God wants from you. If you join the church, learn the secret handshake, and pay the membership dues, you too can find your way.

Anyone who tells you they have all the answers is either lying or selling something.

God does not expect you to fear Him in the sense we use the word. God may expect you to be in awe, but "awe" is not fear, though they come from the same word and are both used in the Scriptures. To be in awe of God is not to fear Him. In the Connection of the Soul, we are told to recognize that God is God and that you are not. That isn't fear either.

Perhaps the fear He's looking for is the kind you feel while playing hide and seek. When my children were young, perhaps five and six, I would pretend to be asleep on the couch, and when they would come close, I would jump up and scream and then wrestle them to the ground. It became a game. They would inch up closer and closer, knowing I was going to jump up but still creeping closer all the time. That was a different kind of fear. That was fear born in love.

But if a father demands fear in order to get love, that's dysfunction. That's abuse. God is not like that.

Brother Lawrence refers to the "person of piety." One has to wonder what the person of piety was doing visiting the humble brother. Persons of piety often like to visit those they look down on and believe they can influence or impress with their knowledge. I picture Brother Lawrence nodding and smiling and trying to understand where this person was coming from.

The simple answers are the best. "I am God's."

Pray that prayer today. Sometime before your head hits the pillow tonight, pray that simple prayer, "God, I am Yours." The results could be astounding.

Objects in the Rearview Mirror

As for what passes in me at present, I cannot express it. I have no pain or difficulty about my state, because I have no will but that of God, which I endeavor to accomplish in all things, and to which I am so resigned that I would not take up a straw from the ground against His order, or from any other motive than purely that of love to Him.
—Brother Lawrence

God has put you in the place you are for a reason. You might not be able to see it now, but you will. Those hard days are making you stronger. Maybe you aren't ready for what you want yet. Maybe what you are about to move into isn't ready yet, so God is just going to keep you where you are for the time being until all things are ready.

Scars heel. That's how we build muscle. There is tearing and healing, and muscles form over the scar. The practice of the presence teaches us that this is all part of living for the will of God. Brother Lawrence was able to see that. He didn't consider his pains or his bad days a problem because he knew he was part of something bigger.

It is not God's will that you suffer. It is God's will that you grow.

My friend Al says that God will speak to us in one of two ways. God will whisper in our ear or smack us upside the head with a brick. We can either listen for the whisper or wait for the brick. It's our choice.

Once we learn to connect with God, His will becomes clearer. Not all the time, and sometimes not very much, but a little. If we are following the will of God, we will feel that union of the soul, and we will know whether or not God wants us to pick up that straw or just let it go.

Hammer and Chisel

As for my set hours of prayer, they are only a continuation of the same exercise. Sometimes I consider myself there as a stone before a carver, whereof he is to make a statue; presenting myself thus before God, I desire Him to form His perfect image in my soul, and make me entirely like Himself. —Brother Lawrence

Years ago I was a wedding date for a beautiful girl who later became my beautiful wife. In fact, you pretty much know you love someone when you go along to the wedding of two people you don't know. So I was the tag-along date. During the reception I wandered through the church grounds. There were a number of statues in the garden, but one in particular struck me. It was a life-size statue of Jesus. Usually you see Jesus statues with His head raised and His arms out, but this one was different. This one was of Jesus the carpenter. This Jesus had His sleeves rolled up. In one hand He held a mallet and in the other a chisel. His arms were huge, as I would expect for a carpenter in those days. What struck me most was that if you stood in front of the statue, He looked right at you. As if He were studying you like a giant block of wood. You were the uncarved block, and here was the carpenter about to go to work.

Brother Lawrence understood that this is how we go to God. We go to God as the uncarved block and ask Him to go to work.

Don't think for a moment that the hammer and the chisel aren't going to hurt. They are going to hurt like hell. But when we ask God to make out of us what He wills, we are often asking for pain.

There are things about us that we don't need, but we can't see them because we are not the artist. We are the block of wood. Hard. Steady. Immovable. Jesus is going to help us take off what we don't need.

He's going to chisel off the pain and regret we hold onto. He's going to help us let go of the things we've held onto for so long that they have become a part of us. Don't think it's not going to hurt. However, usually that hurt comes from us trying to hang onto something we don't need. If we are willing to simply give it up, the process will become much less painful. At the end we stand before the sculptor ... His creation. The presence of God is not all fun and games. It might be a lesson. It might hurt. God will make His presence known to those who open up and allow themselves to be carved.

Shhh ... It's a Secret

We have a God who is infinitely gracious and knows all about our wants. I always thought that He would reduce you to extremity. He will come in His own time, and when you least expect it. —Brother Lawrence

I knew a guy a few years back whose parents stunned him one night by telling him they were getting a divorce. They had kept their arguments quiet and private. They had never allowed their children to see anything bad or unhappy. They had both put on really-honey-nothing-is-wrong faces for years. Then one night his mother took him out to supper and told him that his dad wasn't coming home anymore.

I met this kid six or eight years later when he was in his early twenties. He hated surprises. He hated to have things kept from him. Talking behind his back made him angry. Secrets put him in a rage.

We often feel like God is keeping something from us. As if God is up there in heaven gathering His angels and saying, "Look what happens when I shake this guy's life up a bit," and they all giggle at our plight.

I don't believe God works that way. Some people will make a great effort to find out what they are getting for Christmas. Others have the willpower to wait and see. When we were children, everything was magical. Stuff "appeared" on holidays with your name on it. Lost teeth could turn into cash. Puppets were real people. Mom really did know everything, and Dad was the strongest guy in the world.

God is a parent. He knows what you need and when you need it. God knows what you can handle right now and what you can't. God knows where you are going to be and how you are being prepared for it. It's under control. We have to stop the fighting and fussing simply because there are things that we don't know. Of course there are things you don't know. If you knew everything, then you would be God. (I'll give you a moment to stop and ponder that thought with the sheer horror that it deserves.)

God already knows. (Now think about that one.)

God already knows what you are going through. God already knows how it's going to work out. We should take comfort in the fact that the Creator of the universe is fully aware of our problems and actually has a plan. Instead we fight and swing our fists in the air in sheer frustration. How can you hear God when you are doing that? How can you possibly connect that way? Stop straining. Breathe deep. God already knows, and eventually you will get to open your presents.

Dangerous Air Bubbles

Hope in Him more than ever; thank Him with me for the favors He does you, particularly for the fortitude and patience which He gives you in your afflictions. It is a plain mark of the care He takes of you. Comfort yourself, then, with Him, and give thanks for all. —Brother Lawrence

A potter sits at his wheel. He molds the clay in his hands, squeezing it and rolling it. He smashes the clay against the wheel and pries it up again, repeating the process over and over. The potter knows that he must "get the bubbles out."

A wire is stretched on the side of the wheel. The potter takes the clay ball he has formed and cuts it in half using the wire. There in the center of the clay is a tiny pocket of air. He studies it, then presses it with his thumb, and begins to work the clay again, harder this time. The potter knows that the clay is going to go through the fire. If a clay vase goes into the fire with an air bubble, it could explode and take out other pieces around it. He's grateful he caught it.

Soon the clay is ready and is placed on the wheel. The hands of the artist build it up slowly and carefully. A metal tool with a sharp edge is used to cut off excess or unneeded bits. Finally the piece is finished. Still wet and fragile, it is gently lifted from the wheel and given a chance to dry before it goes through the fire.

God is the potter. We are the clay.

Your sufferings are not sufferings if you see them as merely part of the process of becoming the vase that God wants you to be. You are made stronger. If you went through the fire as the person you are now, you could not survive and would probably wind up taking others out with you when you crashed and burned.

God is making you stronger. You will never be placed in a situation that you cannot handle. God would achieve no benefit in that. God will not allow you to experience pain because He wants to torment you. You are His creation. Why would He want to destroy you? God does not gain by your flameout.

Thank Him for His gentle touch as He forms what you will be. Thank Him for His presence and the watchful eye of the artist. Thank Him for the strength that He gives you to endure what you are going through. Have faith that He is seeing what we will be when we can only see what we are.

Think and Thank

Let him then think of God the most he can. Let him
accustom himself, by degrees, to this small but holy
exercise. No one will notice it, and nothing is easier than to
repeat often in the day these little internal adorations.
—Brother Lawrence

Thank you, God, for that obnoxious song on the
alarm clock.
Thank you, God, for the feel of the carpet.
Thank you, God, for hot water.
Thank you, God, for the smell of shampoo in the hair
I still have.
Thank you, God, for clean towels.
Thank you, God, for Pop-Tarts and chocolate milk.
Thank you, God, for the cold air in my lungs.
Thank you, God, for this old car. I no longer have to
ride the bus.
Thank you, God, for the drive-through at Starbucks.
Thank you, God, for this parking space at this job I
don't like.
Thank you, God, for the paycheck that pays almost all
my bills.
Thank you, God, for the elevator so I don't have to
climb the stairs.
Thank you, God, for my coworkers who make
me laugh.
Thank you, God, for coffee and yesterday's doughnuts.
Thank you, God, for the friends I have lunch with.
Thank you, God, for the support they give me.

Thank you, God, for the end of the workday.
Thank you, God, for the sunset.
Thank you, God, for traffic reporters, ambulance drivers, traffic cops, and every other job I could never do.
Thank you, God, for letting me spend my evenings with the person I most want to be with.
Thank you, God, for DVDs when there's nothing but junk on television.
Thank you, God, for mint toothpaste.
Thank you, God, for clean sheets, warm blankets, soft pillows.
Thank you, God, for this day.
We'll talk again tomorrow.

Are you starting to get the idea?

Think and thank. Think of what you have been given. Think of all you have. Think of all you can achieve. Then thank God because it's all from Him.

Spiritual Dope Slap

If sometimes he is a little too much absent from that divine presence, God presently makes Himself to be felt in his soul to recall him, which often happens when he is most engaged in his outward business. He answers with exact fidelity to these inward drawings, either by an elevation of his heart toward God, or by a meek and fond regard to Him.
—Brother Lawrence

I have a friend named Marjorie. She's an Episcopal

priest in the Washington, D.C. area. Marjorie works with little kids, and to say she is gifted by God in this regard is an understatement.

Since she started as a clergy, Marjorie has always wanted to be the rector of her own church. She loves working with kids, but she was torn between staying in children's ministry and moving into something else.

She found herself in the National Cathedral talking about this "torn" feeling with a bishop that she knew. As they were talking, she heard a voice behind her say "REV. MADGE!" She turned to see a five-year-old running toward her and then becoming airborne. He leaped into her arms and hugged her tightly. Apparently, the child's mother had some business at the cathedral that day. Marjorie talked with the child and introduced him to the bishop. She then set the child down, and he ran back to his mother, happy to have seen his own priest someplace other than the school building.

Marjorie turned back to the bishop and said, "So, as I was saying, I don't really know what direction God is wanting me to go. I just really feel ..."

At this point the bishop applied a gentle loving dope slap to the side of the younger priest's head and said, "Marjorie, we call that a sign."

There are times when God will feel further than the moon and times when God will feel closer than your skin (thank you, David Crowder, for that line). But in times when you don't feel God is near, is that His fault or yours? If you don't feel God's presence, who moved?

God will make Himself known to you. God will find a way to communicate with you through all of the walls you build with your daily life. We can stand in line at a crowded fast-food restaurant, cell phone in one hand, PalmPilot in the other, the Muzak above us drowning out the music we have on our iPod. We can be thinking about the meeting we just left and the one we have to be at in an hour. Suddenly we think ... why doesn't God talk to me?

Sometimes listening for God is as simple as shutting up. God can lift your spirit or show you some outward and visible sign that He is still there.

Listen.
Watch.
Open.
Believe.

Another Brick in the Wall

Yes, we often stop this torrent by the little value we set upon it. But let us stop it no more; let us enter into ourselves and break down the bank which hinders it. Let us make way for grace; let us redeem the lost time, for perhaps we have but little left. Death follows us close; let us be well prepared for it; for we die but once, and a miscarriage there is irretrievable. —Brother Lawrence

Somewhere in that alternate reality that only exists in books such as this one, there is a beach house. Like all objects of beauty, it has a name. This beach house is called life.

As you wander through the rooms and out the back door, you see that the ocean comes up to the beach and is held back by a giant brick wall. Literally millions of bricks hold the water at bay.

You stand on the balcony and then venture down to the beach. As you approach, you find yourself in the shade of this wall. Walk up close. Each brick is carved painstakingly with words and pictures. This one, the first one you see, is that argument you had with someone about the dishes in the sink; this one is a picture of your face screaming at the car in front of you that was only doing ten miles an hour over the speed limit. This one down here, by your knees ... that was when she said that horrible thing. You begin to see your life laid out like a Hollywood storyboard. Some of the bricks are blank; they haven't been carved with an image yet.

You put your face up close to this wall; behind it you hear the ocean. A single drop has managed to work its way through the miniscule cracks; you touch that water and feel a warmth surge through you. Not heat or temperature but warmth that seems to radiate from within.

Closely, with your nose almost touching the surface, you begin to follow the mortar, looking for other drops dripping down from other cracks. Finally, you find a crack where the water seems to be dripping freely, almost enough to fill a small cup if you could stand there all day and catch it. You touch the water coming down and again feel that strange warmth in your heart. The bricks nearby the crack show that week when it was all so clear. More scenes of you angry, vengeful, hurt, and depressed surround those bricks, and they are in solid foundation. They are not letting anything through.

You find a stone on the beach and carry it back to the spot where the leak is. You begin to scratch the mortar, scrape, carve, dig. In an hour more water streams through. Not a lot, but a little. With each drop you are filled with the love of God.

You can stand here and scrape and scratch and get a little more, but how long would that take? Look up there on the beach, back toward the beach house that is life. See the old guy in the beach chair? He has one of those drinks with an umbrella sticking out of it. He's holding out a sledge hammer for you.
Are you ready for the flood?

Rest

We must, nevertheless, always work at it, because not to advance in the spiritual life is to go back. But those who have the gale of the Holy Spirit go forward even in sleep. If the vessel of our soul is still tossed with winds and storms, let us awake the Lord, who reposes in it, and He will quickly calm the sea. —Brother Lawrence

Imagine the greatest rest stop in the world. You are on a road trip, and the drive is long and hard. You are out of munchies. You've listened to that one CD too many times, and all the radio stations are sounding the same.

This rest stop has a gift shop the size of a mall. Everything is on sale. The food looks great. Fresh fruit and sandwiches instead of overpriced vending machine cheese-and-peanut-butter crackers.

There's a guy standing nearby with a guitar, playing music. He's good. He's selling CDs for $5 each. The bathrooms are immaculate. You buy a sandwich and a slice of fresh apple pie. You sit on a clean bench and listen to the man sing. You plan to get a CD for the road ...

Are you going to stop and think, "This is so nice, maybe I'll just spend all my vacation here"? No. You are going to rest and then continue on. Brother Lawrence said that to stop moving forward, even if you are really, really comfortable, is to move backward. The longer you stay at this rest stop, the closer you are to where you started.

One of the hardest things in the world is to move on. To get back in the car and keep driving even though you know you have a longer drive ahead of you than you do behind you. But you keep going anyway.

You may have noticed as you begin to live the spiritual life that the little things don't bother you like they did. The life you are living is just fine. You start to think, "Yeah, this is good. I can stay here." But you can't. Just like you can't stay at the rest stop, you can't stop during your spiritual journey. The presence of God is a continuing process. You keep going. You keep trying. You keep connecting because that is simply what you have to do. If the threat that you could wind up back where you started isn't enough, then the goal of what you could become should be.

The road hurts. There's construction. There are long delays. A drunk driver is weaving in and out of cars, just missing your bumper before cutting back into the lane and avoiding a head-on collision.

So you pop in your new CD. The voice fills your car and eases your aching shoulders. The melody is sweet, and you start to sing along.

Price Tag

I know that for the right practice of it the heart must be empty of all other things, because God will possess the heart alone; *and as He cannot possess it alone without emptying it of all besides, so neither can He act there, and do in it what He pleases, unless it be left vacant to Him.*
—Brother Lawrence

What are you willing to give up for this whole presence of God thing? Most of us can say we will give up the things that we know are bad for us. You want me to live a pure life? Yeah, I can do that. No more swearing, cheating, drinking. Gone. No problem. By comparison, addiction is easy. I don't say that to belittle the work and struggle some people have gone through to put their lives back together. But there are other things ...

Are you willing to give up pain? You think, sure, I can give up pain. But there is pain deep inside. Someone hurt you a long time ago. Someone did or said something, and you've just held onto it for years. For some reason, it's so satisfying.

Can you give up anger? Can you forgive as Jesus did? Can you forgive the ones who hurt you the most? Most of us will stew over the jerk who got our drive-through order wrong. We'll vow never to go back to that restaurant ever! Can you forgive the ones who hurt you deep in your soul and wrecked your life and damaged you forever? Can you forgive that?

Can you make room for God even if He says, "I need you over here," and it means quitting and working somewhere else for a while? Can you follow God if He points and says, "You, you are a minister"?

Are you willing to give up ego? Can you move yourself and your own desires for what you want from your life and let God move in? Can you put aside those things that convince you that you can handle all this by yourself?

Can you let go of pride? Can you stand up and say, "I need help with this"?

Can you let go of safety? Can you step out on the metal I-beam at the top of the skyscraper with nothing under you and nothing to hold onto?

Can you let go of fear? Can you take the risk to get hurt again even when the last two times left you feeling completely crushed and brokenhearted?

Can you let go of fame? Wealth? The past? The future?

Everybody Wins

There is not in the world a kind of life more sweet and delightful than that of a continual conversation with God. Those only can comprehend it who practice and experience it; yet I do not advise you to do it from that motive. It is not pleasure which we ought to seek in this exercise; but let us do it from a principle of love, and because God would have us. —Brother Lawrence

Have you ever played a game in a group of people and just had a great time? Have you ever had a game ruined by someone who was a rotten loser? Or a rotten winner?

We live in a time and a place where it is not uncommon to have parents banned from their children's sporting events. Kids know how to "play." They know it is play. They know the sweetness of having fun without keeping score and laughing at the loser.

The practice of the presence of God is like this. It's "sweet and delightful" as Brother Lawrence said, but as soon as we start the practice for our own benefit, we run into a problem. It's like the guy on the team who throws a fit when one of his own players drops an easy one. It stops being fun. The purpose of the game becomes winning instead of playing the game.

Years ago I was a summer camp counselor. There was a volleyball net near the dining hall, and in the early evenings groups would gather together and play until the sun went down and you couldn't see the ball until it hit you in the face. One of the other counselors and I noticed that the games were getting too competitive—that it was no longer enough to win the game, you had to win by spiking the ball in front of the weakest player. So we devised a system that when a team rotated, the server had to move to the other team. At first, the kids were furious. They didn't want to play that way. But after a few bouts of a player or two trying to sabotage the game, we soon saw both teams mixed and matched on both sides of the net. Something happened. They laughed more. They spent more time setting the ball up for each other and grandstanded less. They helped each other up from the ground when they fell.

The practice of the presence of God works just like this. We live this life because it is sweet to do so. When we start using the presence to correct others or push our own agenda, we become the spoiled little kid who takes his ball and goes home.

I'm convinced that God smiles on the Special Olympics, a competition that is designed where the goal is playing the game. Sure, it's a competition, and there are gold medals for those who score the best, but perhaps the true reward is that at the end of each lane in the foot race is someone waiting to hug everyone who plays. Everybody runs. Everybody finishes. Everybody wins.

One

It is, however, necessary to put our whole trust in God, laying aside all other cares, and even some particular forms of devotion, though very good in themselves, yet such as one often engages in unreasonably, because these devotions are only means to attain to the end. So when by this exercise of the presence of God we are with Him *who is our end, it is then useless to return to the means; but we may continue with Him our commerce of love, persevering*

*in His holy presence, one while by an act of praise, of
adoration, or of desire; one while by an act of resignation
or thanksgiving; and in all the ways which our spirit can
invent.* —Brother Lawrence

Is it possible to be a worship addict? We all strive to
find those God moments, but what happens when
they become the goal instead of the presence?

Many smaller churches wish they could grow to
the megachurch size. They want the 5,000-seat
auditorium instead of the 250-seat sanctuary. What
if we are supposed to grow the other way? The act
of "practicing the presence" is an intimate one not a
corporate one. Shouldn't things be flipped around?

The corporate megachurch is the place to start, and
then as we grow and mature in our faith, should we
not begin attending the smaller churches?

When we begin attending church for the "social"
aspect ... When we begin attending church for that
rock-concert feeling ... When we begin attending
church because it makes us feel good to be in the
audience ...

We have allowed the "means" to come before the end.
Brother Lawrence taught us that God is the end. We
are to worship Him and not worship ourselves.

That's not to say that there is something wrong
with three-story speakers and a state-of-the-art

PowerPoint system. These would fall under what the good brother means by "acts of praise or adoration."

But we must also look at "acts of resignation." We can deny ourselves the sound, the band, the light show, and simply look for God within. Praying to connect with the God who is deep within us already rather than praying to connect with the God who is out there someplace.

It's like reading a children's book, which is short and designed with pictures. When we get older, we don't need the cardboard pages with clocks and fabric and noisemakers. We can pick up a novel, and all the action can take place in our minds.

Perhaps the key phrase is "all manner in which the spirit can invent."

We must practice the presence of God in our heats and minds and souls. However you connect ... CONNECT.

Sabbath

It is not necessary for being with God to be always at church. We may make an oratory of our heart wherein to retire from time to time to converse with Him in meekness, humility, and love. Every one is capable of such familiar conversation with God, some more, some less. He knows what we can do. Let us begin, then. —Brother Lawrence

Yes! Yes! Yes! I can sleep in on Sunday mornings!
Ah, well, not exactly.

I moved into a new house last June. Part of the
attraction was that this house has something I've
always wanted ... a back porch.

There are just a few Sundays mornings during the year
when I will not be in church. On those days I like to
get a dozen doughnuts, a cup of coffee, and a crisp
Sunday *New York Times*, put my feet up on my back
porch, and enjoy my morning. This is one of the most
pleasurable things in the world to me.

Worship is important. There are Scriptures
throughout the Bible that talk about the importance
of gathering. "We gather together to ask the Lord's
blessing" ... as the favorite hymn goes.

Brother Lawrence wrote that we should occasionally
take time out from worship and use that time to be
alone with God.

It's the "familiar conversation with God" that throws
most people. Brother Lawrence said that anyone is
capable of achieving this, some more and some less.

Instead of saying she prays, my friend Julie says, "I
crawled up in God's lap, and we had a talk." I have
always been amazed at people who feel that at
home in God's presence. When Jesus prayed to His
Father for His disciples toward the end of His life,

the Scriptures tell us that He used the very informal "Abba," which in essence means "daddy." Saint Paul tells us that we should be calling God "daddy" as well.

Our Daddy who art in heaven. where sin revolts suicidal that ap day-

Does it sound right to you? Me neither, but Brother Lawrence said that is the goal. That is what we are trying to achieve with the practice of the presence— to eventually have a relationship with God that is so informal that we call Him "daddy."

It is also worth noting that Brother Lawrence said everyone is capable of this kind of relationship. Everyone. You. Me. Those people whose beliefs and theology we would spend a lifetime arguing were wrong (people who live in the red states, people who live in the blue states, people who call during the dinner hour to sell you a water softener, people who take cell phone calls in the movie theater, people who put bombs in schools).

The "meekness and humility" throw people off too. Approach God humbly. Approach God gently. Do you think that the people who pray at full volume in the restaurant pray that loudly when they sit down to eat a tuna sandwich in their kitchens?

God already knows what you need. You aren't giving Him any new information when you pray. So let's chill out a little. Ask God how His day went. Thank Him for the day He gave you—even if it's a bad day.

Jewish men wear a prayer shawl called a *talis*; it is not for warmth like a shawl your grandmother wears. This shawl is to cover or envelop the one praying. When Jesus said to "go into your prayer closet," He wasn't talking about a physical room or meditation chamber. He was referring to when men would drape their talis over their heads and arms creating a sort of tent.

Worship at full volume if that is what makes God real for you, but it would seem that practicing the presence of God also requires time alone in the prayer closet where it is just you and God.

Listen

Accustom yourself, then, by degrees thus to worship Him, to beg His grace, to offer Him your heart from time to time in the midst of your business, even every moment, if you can. Do not always scrupulously confine yourself to certain rules, or particular forms of devotion, but act with a general confidence in God. —Brother Lawrence

God is listening. God is listening to the soloist who is quietly singing "Just as I Am" in the back of the sanctuary at the Full Gospel Pentecostal Church on Route 2 in Barnbow, Mississippi. God is listening to the child reciting the week's memory verse in a Methodist Sunday school. God is listening.

God wants to talk with you. We've spent a lot of time talking about how we should approach God informally ... like in a conversation. Shouldn't we also be willing to listen the same way?

Remember the beginning of *Monty Python and the Holy Grail*? God appears in the cloud, and the Knights of the Round Table fall to their knees and avert their eyes. And God says: "Oh, don't grovel. If there's one thing I can't stand, it's people groveling. And don't apologize. Every time I want to talk to someone, it's 'sorry this' or 'forgive me that' or 'I'm not worthy.' Knock it off!"

What is God's part in this informal presence? We talked about what God said when Job started to complain. "Did you put the stars in place?" But if we recognize that God is God, shouldn't we then be able to just talk?

Have you ever had lunch with a professor or your boss? We recognize that complete and total authority, but it's possible to have a conversation as well.

We say "thank God" a lot.

"That report is due next week not tomorrow." Oh thank God.

"The boss is running late." Oh thank God.

"There's one pint of Chocolate Brownie left." Oh thank God.

But do we really thank God? "Dear God, thank you for leaving one last pint of my favorite Ben & Jerry's flavor. It was a bad day, and I really need this." How much time does that take out of our busy lives?

If you are driving home from work and find yourself sitting under the electronic road warning sign: "Construction Next Twenty Miles—Expect Delays," use that time to talk to God. Yeah, you may look silly to those around you, but no sillier than those who talk on a headset cell phone or sing along with Mariah Carey on the radio.

A conversation takes two. If you want to hear God, you have to do your part.

Speak

I believe one remedy for this is to confess our faults and to humble ourselves before God. I do not advise you to use multiplicity of words in prayer, many words and long discourses being often the occasions of wandering. Hold yourself in prayer before God like a dumb or paralytic beggar at a rich man's gate. Let it be your business to keep your mind in the presence of the Lord. —Brother Lawrence

Words to leave out of a prayer:

Thou
Wouldst
Thee
Twas
Dost
Ye
Bless-ED

God Is Here

Reign
Thine
Forsake

Some people can pray off the cuff. They are the ones who get asked to pray at meals and around campfires. Words just seem to flow out of them, and it sounds like poetry. Others pray like they just spent the day reading the thesaurus. But some of us can't pray our way out of a paper bag, and we like to have our prayers and blessings written down.

I once knew a man at the first church I ever worked at who objected to prayers being written in the bulletin. "If a man doesn't know what he wants to say to his Creator, then let him sit down and think a little harder."

If we go to God and say:

Lo, oh Heavenly Father, maker of heaven and earth, do not forsake me, a poor sinner who did grieve Thou by my actions.

You think God is not going to know, "Hey, I screwed up on this one."

Flowering a pile of horse manure isn't going to make it less of a pile of horse manure.

God is not impressed with your vocabulary. He's going to look at your heart and see if you mean the prayer. Do your actions back up the words? Or do you think by using impressive church talk that God is going to give you a pass on this one?

God is going to give you the pass anyway. That's grace. But would you go to your roommate and say "Lo, forgive me in thy gentle mercy for I didst take the last can of Diet Pepsi while thou wert at thy place of employment"?

Then don't go to God that way either.

Focus

If [your mind] sometimes wander and withdraw itself from Him, do not much disquiet yourself for that: trouble and disquiet serve rather to distract the mind than to recollect it; the will must bring it back in tranquillity. If you persevere in this manner, God will have pity on you.
—Brother Lawrence

Have you ever wanted the ability to read minds?

I have this theory that the mind wanders more in church than anywhere else. We think about the cobwebs on the ceiling. We think about where we are going for lunch. One thought leads to another, and we find ourselves a thousand miles away.

When we were kids, this sort of thing earned us an elbow from mom. As adults, we may get the elbow from our spouse, or they may just let us sit there slack-jawed and spaced out, much to the amusement of the choir.

Brother Lawrence said, "Don't beat yourself up over it."

Ever worry about slipping and falling when you step into the bathtub? Does it run through your mind when you are walking on ice? Very often it's not the fall that gets us hurt; it's what we do to try not to hurt ourselves. It's very possible that you can hurt your back worse twisting to keep from falling than if you just fall flat in the first place.

Trying to steer your way out of a skid once the car starts spinning produces the same result. We make things worse when we try to fix the problem. That's something that applies to just about any place in life.

Brother Lawrence believed that "disquieting" ourselves, or beating ourselves up for letting our minds wander, only serves to distance us even further from God at that moment.

God is not going to squash you like a bug because you are trying to make "cloud pictures" out of the water stain on the ceiling. God gave you the brain that's taking you in that direction.

If the last hymn starts and you suddenly realize that you've been "away," don't think yourself any less a Christian. It happens. Focus your mind on what you're doing and do that. This is the way the mind works. I can write phrases like ...

Hot Fudge
Comfy Chair
Monty Python
Michael Jackson
Dr Pepper
Yippee-ky-eye-yea

And your mind can conjure dozens of images and thoughts that can spark other ideas and those will spark still more. That's how the brain works. If we are made in the image of God, perhaps His mind wanders as well.

When He's in heaven listening to some of the most moronic prayers and "props" from rap stars accepting awards, I imagine He has a favorite place His mind wanders to as well.

Bring your mind back to what's in front of you and start again. God understands.

Far, Far Away

One way to recollect the mind easily in the time of prayer, and preserve it more in tranquillity, is not to let it wander too far at other times. *You should keep it strictly in the presence of God; and being accustomed to think of Him often, you will find it easy to keep your mind calm in the time of prayer, or at least to recall it from its wanderings.*
—Brother Lawrence

OK, so how do we keep from letting our minds wander during church in the first place? Start by not letting it wander too far at other times.

Every now and then, I realize that I've driven all the way to work and I barely remember the drive. Yeah, that sounds like I should have my license taken away, doesn't it? But, honestly, have you ever sat in a large auditorium classroom or been doing homework and suddenly just snapped back to attention? We can have a pile of papers in front of us and get distracted by the construction going on outside our window. We come back to reality (hopefully) before the boss walks by our door.

There are occupations where this sort of thing could be a plus, but for the average Joe in his average office in the average job making average money, a little more concentration is expected.

A little more focus during the rest of the week will help you keep your mind where it needs to be during the worship service.

Focus on God. People say, "I don't go to church because it's booooring." It might be for someone who isn't paying attention.

You will get out of a worship experience what you put into a worship experience. You will get out of a relationship what you put into it. If you sit back and say, "What have you done for me lately?" it's not going to last that long.

Worshiping God is like doing the "Hokey Pokey."
You put your whole self in. If you place your body in
the pew and then leave when the service is over, you
didn't get what it was all about.

We have to put everything into it. Heart. Mind. Body.
Soul. Our whole selves. This is what Brother Lawrence
was talking about with the presence. We cannot
experience the connection (the way God intended)
unless we are willing to go all the way with it. Commit
yourself to staying in the game, and you will reap the
benefits.

Is this difficult? Yes. Does it take practice? Yes. Will it
get easier? Yes.

You are not going to do any activity ... sports, dance,
yoga, Aikido ... the first time you try. You must stretch.
You must practice. You must try to do a little better
each time.

The practice of the presence of God is no different.

Not Alone

*We cannot escape the dangers which abound in life without
the actual and* continual *help of God. Let us, then, pray to
Him for it continually. How can we pray to Him without
being with Him? How can we be with Him but in thinking
of Him often? And how can we often think of Him but by
a holy habit which we should form of it? You will tell me
that I am always saying the same thing. It is true, for this is*

the best and easiest method I know; and as I use no other, I advise all the world to do it. We must know before we can love. In order to know God, we must often think of Him; and when we come to love Him, we shall also think of Him often, for our heart will be with our treasure.
—Brother Lawrence

Life is hard. Less so (in degrees) for those who believe. But only if you pray. You can't pray to God if you don't know God. You can't know God if you don't think about God ... all the time. You can't think about God unless you decide to ... all the time. Then thinking of God becomes subconscious. The presence of God becomes natural. Life is still hard. But you can deal with it.

I want to be a singer. I want to stand on that stage and belt out a song that has them cheering. I want the accolades and financial reward that go along with being a singer at the top of his game.

But ... I don't want to practice. I don't want to be a better singer than I am now. I don't want to learn about music. I don't want to hear different kinds of music. I really don't like music all that much. But I really do want to be in the spotlight. Yeah, like that's going to happen.

How can you connect to the presence of God if you don't even bother thinking about God? How can you find that peace of soul that Brother Lawrence talked about if God only occurs to you when you see one of those television preachers in flamboyant suits?

Make it a habit. Pray each morning. As you ready yourself for work, put the 8:45 a.m. board meeting out of your mind and concentrate on God. Do this every morning. Make a conscious effort to pray—not for things, not even for yourself, but just a quiet praise or thanks without "thees and thous." When this becomes habit, start praying as you drive.

"Ponder" is an underrated word. To mull over, to contemplate, to wonder about, to consider. Ponder on God. Think of the whys, wheres, hows, and whos of God. Don't push for answers or solutions. Just ponder God.

You cannot love someone you do not know. Relationships fail based on this principle. You cannot love someone you have not met, talked with, communicated with. The same goes for God.

We can never know all of God (He is too much), but we can know God enough. We cannot know any of God if we do not communicate. We cannot know God if we do not allow Him to know us. If we shut God out at every opportunity or if we ask that God come and be with us on our schedule, then we may as well turn Him away altogether.

Every Day

Pray remember what I have recommended to you, which is, to think often on God, by day, by night, in your business, and even in your diversions. He is always near you and with you; leave Him not alone. You would think it rude to leave a friend alone who came to visit you; why, then, must God be neglected? Do not, then, forget Him, but think on Him often, adore Him continually, live and die with Him; this is the glorious employment of a Christian. In a word, this is our profession; if we do not know it, we must learn it.
—Brother Lawrence

Your best friend is coming into town. You haven't seen her in years. Are you going to get to the airport "whenever" and maybe wash the sheets in the guest room? You might provide some bread and peanut butter while she is there, and if you decide to stay at home that weekend, you might go out and do something, but who knows? No.

You'll clean your car before you go to the airport. You'll make sure the house is clean. You'll go and get all of her favorite junk foods and fill your cupboards. You'll put flowers in the guest room. You'll rent a bunch of cool DVDs from Blockbuster. In short, you'll put forth an effort.

We stand up and say, "God, I want You to be a part of my life. I want to know You. I want to see Your face."

What is our obligation if God says, "OK, sure. What are we going to do?"

God doesn't need to go to Blockbuster with you or out for ice cream. God wants to be part of you. God wants that connection that occurs when you practice the presence. To God, that's like a weekend of pizza and movies. The trick is to make it last ...

If I asked you to quickly think of the name of a person who achieved the top of their game professionally, what's the first name that comes to mind: Michael Jordan, Robin Williams, Ray Charles, Bill Gates?

Someone who not only was the best at what they did but set a precedent for everyone else. There are athletes out there who may be considered "the new Michael Jordan" or "the young Michael Jordan" or "the next Michael Jordan," but there will never be "another Michael Jordan."

When Brother Lawrence wrote about "the glorious employment of a Christian" and "this is our profession," I think this is what he was referring to. To be so good at being in the presence of God that we leave a mark. Not for our own egos, but that we can affect the world around us and worlds yet to come by who we are.

Mother Teresa was such a person. She did not evangelize. She did not go into the world and keep a list of her converts or conquests. She simply was in the presence of God and changed the world by existing in it. She was famous but did not seek fame. Any clout she had she used to further the presence of God in the world.

Being a Christian does not mean you have a scorecard. You don't keep notches in your belt. Instead, you want to have an effect on those around you without beating them over the head with a cross and dragging them back to church.

In the same way that we don't have to think about breathing, God is a part of us day and night. We should be all about God.

Make It All Better

I do not pray that you may be delivered from your pains, but I pray God earnestly that He would give you strength and patience to bear them as long as He pleases. Comfort yourself with Him who holds you fastened to the cross. He will loose you when He thinks fit. Happy those who suffer with Him. Accustom yourself to suffer in that manner, and seek from Him the strength to endure as much, and as long, as He shall judge to be necessary for you.
—Brother Lawrence

This one is hard. When we see a loved one in pain, we have no problem hitting our knees and saying, "God, take the pain away," or "God, make it all better," or "God, I promise I'll go to church every Sunday and give 10 percent of my income to the poor if You don't let her die. Please."

Sometimes when we are at the end of the rope and we feel like we are standing knee deep in muck and bugs at the bottom of an emotional well, we will search the skies and say, "God, why is this happening? Get me out of this hole." (Read the Psalms—even David, one of God's main guys, felt like that.)

Brother Lawrence said that part of the connection, part of the practice of the presence of God, is to NOT pray that way.

Don't ask God to fix your problems. For the most part, God doesn't work that way. He fixes some of our problems, but we don't get to know which ones or, more importantly, when.

Don't ask God to heal your broken heart; ask God for the strength to get through another day with a broken heart.

Don't ask God to cure your best friend's cancer; ask God to help your friend deal with the cancer, help ease the pain, help the family move on when the inevitable happens.

When we ask God to intervene and change something about our lives, we usually are doing so out of our own selfish motivation.

We don't want to lose our best friend, so we ask God to heal him. We don't ask what the plan is. We don't say, "Thy will be done." We don't say, "God gives, and God takes away. Blessed be the name of God." That's not how we pray.

Perhaps the overwhelming despair you feel is for a reason. Maybe it's to make you stronger for something else. Maybe the party isn't ready yet, so God is going to leave you down in the well just a little longer until everything is in place.

I have learned that everything is connected to everything else. One event changes a thousand others, and when we push and pull and try to squeeze our own agenda into God's plan, we usually find ourselves back at the bottom of the well.

God is a parent who has no problem sticking your nose in the corner for a while if you don't do what you are told. Be patient. Be still. Know that I am God (Ps. 46).

Pain and Suffering ... Yes!

The men of the world do not comprehend these truths, nor is it to be wondered at, since they suffer like what they are, and not like Christians. They consider sickness as a pain to nature, and not as a favor from God; and seeing it only in that light, they find nothing in it but grief and distress. But those who consider sickness as coming from the hand of God, as the effect of His mercy, and the means which He employs for their salvation—such commonly find in it great sweetness and sensible consolation. —Brother Lawrence

Some people just don't get it.

Some people see hurt and anguish as their lot in life, and they suffer through it, sometimes daily. They think that everyone goes through times of hurt and anguish, and now is just their time.

Some people see their pain as punishment from God. Some sort of divine retribution for something they have done, or perhaps they are still paying off their parent's debt in some sort of trickle-down, sin-billing system.

Some people seem to be getting something out of it. As if the more pain they go through, the more attention and pity they receive, and they confuse this with love.

Those who can only see the pain are missing something.

If we understand that the fire makes the clay stronger ... If we understand that the soil must be tilled before it can be planted ... If we understand that the coal must go through intense pressure before it becomes a diamond ... Then we understand what hurt and anguish are: God's means of making us diamonds.

Brother Lawrence celebrated his pain. If it was God's

wisdom that he hurt, then he would hurt for God. As he grew older, he spent a great deal of time writing about his pain but never once complaining. Never once wishing it away, but still celebrating when it alleviated somewhat.

To thank God for the pain seems wrong to us. But we are a people that looks at our pain and immediately looks for someone to blame it on. It's hard to thank God for the fire when you are burning. But when we are a vase of flowers sitting on God's table, we look back and see what a gift the fire really was.

God Only Knows

God knoweth best what is needful for us, and all that He does is for our good. If we knew how much He loves us, we should always be ready to receive equally and with indifference from His hand the sweet and the bitter. All would please that came from Him. That sorest afflictions never appear intolerable, except when we see them in the wrong light. When we see them as dispensed by the hand of God, when we know that it is our loving Father who abases and distresses us, our sufferings will lose their bitterness and become even matter of consolation.
—Brother Lawrence

Let us ponder for a moment ... Everything is connected to everything else.

Even those who question the existence of God will often concede that there is an order to the universe.

Call it "the cause," call it "higher power," pick a phrase and use it. There is an order to the universe. The psalmist sees it in Psalm 104. Everything fits together. No matter how far out into the universe we look, no matter how deep we look into the world of microbes with microscopes, we see that everything is connected to everything else.

God created all that. God put the universe in place. God made the stream run into the river that runs into the ocean. God put the tree by the river to give shade to the animals and the branches to give a home to the birds.

Now, zoom out with this spiritual camera and see the angels. Beings of light that come and go throughout the Scriptures. These are beings who have touched the face of God. God made them.

With all that, now consider that the closest thing to God in all of creation is you. You are not God; we talked about that, but the closest thing to God that exists is you. You are higher on God's list than His angels. God loves you more than anything.

Why would a God like that want to hurt His favorite creation? There's an old children's ditty that says, "God made the rose, and the devil made the thorn." What a horrible thing to teach children. God also made the thorn—to protect the rose. God created them both.

If a car slides on the ice and bends the fender of the

car in front of it, Satan did not put the ice on the road. There is ice on the road because the snow melted and then froze. God made snow. God made the sun that melted the snow. God made the earth tilt on its axis so we would have the seasons.

The concept of throwing salt over your shoulder started centuries ago because salt was valuable, and if you spilled it, there must be a demon behind you. The idea was to collect the spilled salt and throw it in the eye of whatever "badness" was hanging out over your shoulder.

Everything comes from God. Good and bad (or bitter and sweet, as Brother Lawrence said) come from God.

How different our lives would be if we stopped thinking of bad things as God's punishment for something we did and saw them as gifts from a loving Father who wants us to learn and grow and be kind to each other once in a while.

Getting to Know You

Let all our employment be to know *God; the more one knows Him the more one desires to know Him. And as knowledge is commonly the measure of love, the deeper and more extensive our knowledge shall be, the greater will be our love; and if our love of God were great, we should love Him equally in pains and pleasures.* —Brother Lawrence

Psalm 29—The Voice of God (author's paraphrase)

> Know God.
> Know what it means to belong to God.
> Know that God is all-powerful.
> Know that your mind could not grasp the face
> of God.
> Angels shine for God.
> God's voice is a thunder.
> It rolls across the seas.
> It is a voice of power beyond our
> comprehension.
> God's voice can shatter a forest.
> God's voice can flash like fire.
> God will be God forever.
> There is no end to God.
> May the voice of God grant us strength.
> May the voice of God give us peace.
> Amen.

Think about the first time you started to become passionate about something. Maybe it was music. You wanted to know everything. Not just in an I-really-like-that-song way but in a deep, passionate way. The more you learned about it, the more you wanted to learn about it.

I love listening to the director's commentary tracks on DVDs. Listen to the commentary tracks on a Robert Rodriguez movie, and you will hear the passion he has for his work. You can learn so much about how the movie came together and what he did to make the movie better in ways that the average viewer would never pick up on in a million years.

Do you remember the first time you felt so passionate about something that you had to learn everything, study everything, and then learn more? It was as if there wasn't enough information for you to absorb. You wanted it all.

This is how we should want to know God. How wonderful to find something to be passionate about that would be an infinite source of information. You could never know it all. There would always be more.

Pick up a Bible. Read a book about God. Learn what other religions know that you don't. Look at art. Why did a passionate man lie on his back for years and paint God on a ceiling? Why do some people refer to Beethoven's "Moonlight Sonata" as "God's favorite piece of music"?

The more you learn, the more you want to learn, and the well of information never runs dry.

Brother Lawrence wrote, "Knowledge is the measure of love."

The deeper and more expansive your knowledge of a subject, the deeper and more expansive your love.

Let us have that for God.

Let our love be so deep that it becomes a passion to know Him more. Let our greatest desire be to see God's own face.

If we can make knowing God our passion, then we can begin to see that all things are from Him. Good and bad. Bitter and sweet. It's all from God, and it's all good.

Presents

Let us not content ourselves with loving God for the mere sensible favors, how elevated soever, which He has done or may do us. Such favors, though never so great, cannot bring us so near to Him as faith does in one simple act. Let us seek Him often by faith. He is within us; seek Him not elsewhere. If we do love Him alone, are we not rude, and do we not deserve blame, if we busy ourselves about trifles which do not please and perhaps offend Him?
—Brother Lawrence

Think of your God moments ...

- Standing on top of a building at night and watching the city come alive.

- An open road, an open window, and the perfect driving song on the radio.

- Standing around the campfire with a small group of your friends.

- Holding your first child for the first time.

- Looking down the aisle and seeing the one you are going to marry.

- Hearing the favorite song of a beloved relative sung at their funeral.

These are some of mine ... you have your own. Think on those for a moment. Seriously, put your finger in the book, close your eyes, and think of your God moments.

These are the sensual blessings in that they are of the senses. But none of these will connect us to God even close to the way we can connect with Him in the everyday acts of faith.

- Letting the kid at the lemonade stand keep the change.

- Cutting the student some slack because he was late to class and couldn't help it.

- Giving a can of food to the food drive.

- Donating your old clothes, not for the tax deduction but because people are actually cold.

- Listening to the friend whose boyfriend just dumped her.

- Encouraging the street performer who has a guitar case full of quarters.

- Tutoring the kid who's failing math.

- Skipping your lunch so that someone else can have at least one meal for the day.

- Praising God when the world seems to be falling apart.

- Praying for the health and well-being of a president even if you didn't vote for him.

Let me paint an image for you from *Indiana Jones and the Last Crusade.* It is the end of the movie. Indiana is creeping his way toward the grail because his father lies dying in the anteroom. Now he stands at the entrance to a vast cavern. The door on the opposite side is too far to jump, and there is no way to swing across. He must take a step of faith.

Luckily, God does not expect this of us. Perhaps under the right circumstances, anyone could place their hand on their heart and step out into the abyss with the full faith that they would not then plummet to a painful death, thereby failing the world and their Father.

God calls us to listen when He says, "I'm here." Without evidence, we are asked to believe.

The Last Detail

This is the last known writing of Brother Lawrence. After he completed this letter, he took to his sickbed and died a few days later.

Let us begin to be devoted to Him in good earnest. Let us cast everything besides out of our hearts. He would possess them alone. Beg this favor of Him. If we do what we can on our parts, we shall soon see that change wrought in us which we aspire after. I cannot thank Him sufficiently for the relaxation He has vouchsafed you. I hope from His mercy the favor to see Him with a few days. Let us pray for one another. —Brother Lawrence

We can be different people. We can be better people. We can become the kind of people we want to be.

We cannot accomplish this on our own. Likewise we cannot stand before God and say, "Change me." God will not.

It is through the continued presence that we become who we are.

It is through the *continued* presence that we become anything.

Conclusion

All things are possible
to him who believes,
they are less difficult
to him who hopes,
they are more easy
to him who loves
and still more easy
to him who perseveres
in the practice of
these three virtues.
—Brother Lawrence

Discussion Guide

Week One: The Vision, A Note from the Author, The Biography, God of Pots and Pans (pp. xiii-18)

1. Have you ever had a profound spiritual experience? What was it like? When did it happen? Do you think it's necessary to have this type of experience in order to lead a spiritual life?

2. Brother Lawrence went through a wide variety of jobs before he found his way to the monastery. Do you think everyone is "called" to a certain line of work? Are you currently doing what you think you were meant by God to do? Does your "calling" have to be your employment?

3. Brother Lawrence believed that God was going to punish him for his sins, that he was not good enough or spiritual enough to be loved by God. Do you think it's possible for anyone not to be loved by God? Does God punish us? What does God expect from us?

4. Have you ever gone to God with a sort of "Christmas list" of wants and desires? What happened? Why is God often our last resort after everything else has failed?

5. Are there some activities you consider more spiritual than others? Why? If you thought you were cleaning your house for the glory of God, would it be cleaner or would you just be happier doing it?

Week Two: A Monk's Disclaimer, How to Live a Spiritual Life, How to Love God, Starting This Journey (pp. 21-56)

1. What causes the perception that God is with us at certain times and leaves us on our own at others? What are some ways we can flip that mental switch in our minds and acknowledge that God is present always?

2. When was the last time you prayed? How did you pray when you were a child? Does having a practiced prayer or written prayer help you to pray? Why do we think that some people are heard more than others? Are they? Does God listen to Billy Graham more than He listens to a child molester in prison? Explain.

3. We don't talk to our bosses, grandparents, or preachers the same way we talk to our closest friends. That's because we feel safest and accepted with those we are closest to. Why is it hard to think of God that way? What was the first image of God you remember seeing as a child?

4. What are you doing when you are the most aware of the details around you? Driving? At work? Setting up a romantic date? Watching your children play?

5. When you take a vacation, do you treat it like a job? Do you plan out every detail so that every moment is full or do you plan time for simply sitting by the pool?

Week Three: What Is the Presence?, How to Acquire the Presence, The Benefits of the Presence (pp. 59-93)

1. Do you know someone who seems to always feel comfortable in their own skin? Who is it? How old are they? Do you think it gets easier once you have fifty or sixty years of life experiences? What things do you allow to get in the way of your continued union with God?

2. Why do you think it's hard for some people to believe that God really is interested in spending time with them? How do we take God down off the pedestal and put our arms around Him? When was the last time you felt like you "belonged" to God? What were you doing at the time?

3. What would you do if you said, "Speak, Lord, your servant is listening," and you actually heard something? What would you expect to hear?

4. Think about who you were at age ten. Now think of who you were at fifteen, eighteen, twenty. How have you changed? What is the most significant change you've been through in the last five years?

5. What was your faith like when you were a child? What did they teach you in Sunday school about faith? Have you ever experienced a crisis of faith? How did you come back from that?

Week Four: Gathered Thoughts (pp. 95-192)

1. What are you doing when you feel the most alive? Saint Ignatius said, "That is where God is." What are you doing when you can go for hours and never look at a clock?

2. Have you ever missed God because you were too busy being religious? Talk about a time when God showed up unexpectedly. What is the greatest God moment you've experienced that had nothing to do with church? What is one way that you have made your life ready for God's presence?

3. What is the best thing that has happened to you this week? Have you said "thank you" to God yet? Read the list on page 151 ("Think and Thank") again. Now come up with ten of your own.

4. Have you ever had something bad happen to you and then later found a way to draw on that experience to get through something bigger? Explain.

5. What is something you do every day without even thinking about it? How did you get to a place where it was automatic? What can you do to make prayer that easy?

[RELEVANTBOOKS]

For more information about other Relevant Books,